The Worshipper's Purpose:

a Journey to Knowing Man's Mandate

See you at the top

Bunmi Javia Denton

(Delightsome One)

Endorsements

'Many years in the ministry, has shown me of the need to worship God sincerely and what happens when we do this. What Bunmi Denton has brought in this book is words to guide, birthed through her walk with God, her experiences with Him, through her many years as a worship leader and through her practice in her time of personal worship.

This book which is a required reading for every child of God, will help us discern 'Why I'm here' and how to worship the God that makes it possible. After all John 4:24 says 'God is Spirit, and those who worship Him must worship in spirit and truth.'

Read and be blessed.'

Pastor (Mrs) Bambo Amachree
President Women in His Presence (WIHP) Ministry

'The act of praise and worship is an important part of one's walk with God. This book will inspire you and help you build that aspect of your walk with God daily and through your life as the book is an eye opener to the secret of the act of praise and worship.'

Dr Pastor Shola Jordan Adeoye
Peculiar vision International

'The area of worship is a vital area in the church that's not been touched for ages because people don't really understand the true meaning of what it is to worship God in Spirit and in Truth. We have been chosen to worship and made to worship God in all areas of our lives. Minister Bunmi has been able to show in depth through this ground breaking book the truths behind worship and what it means to be a worshipper.'

Pastor Tunji Olujimi — Pastor/Worship Leader and Book Author Coach
Glory Realm Ministries and T.O Consultancy

'It is indeed a privilege to endorse your book which was also birthed out of the Prophetic. I remember giving you the prophetic word while in Seville that you will be launching your first book in November. You gazed at me. Now look and see what the Lord has done. I am so happy and feel privileged to do an endorsement with Reverend Dapo Adegboyega. It is a great achievement, congratulations!'

Mama Blessing Asanya
DOZ Ministries

'Worship is our God-given and God-commanded mandate. The Bible carries records of many people who genuinely worshipped God and had their breakthrough; from Abraham's servant in genesis 24 verses26, 48 & 52 to revelation 14: 7, and the word 'worship' popping up 188 times. Worship is what translates us from the outer court to the holy of holies (innermost sanctuary — psalm 28:2 & Hebrews 9:8 — amplified bible).

This book penned by minister Bunmi Denton is a worshipper's manual. It is a tool for everyone who wants to get to God's throne room in order to download their purpose, from the Master. In this worshipper's purpose book, we can discover and uncover our destiny if we can learn the rudiments of genuine worship, prescribed in this book's contents.

Minister Bunmi has taken time to search and unlock God's greatest need and the pathway to delivering this great need, which is pure worship. I have no hesitation in recommending this book to all who are searching for the reason of their being. Without doubt, this great piece of work will be a blessing to millions across the globe.'

Pastor Richard Oluwawo
Rccg House of the Lord South Ockendon UK

Contents

Foreword

If there was ever a time in history when everyone needs to hear from God directly and have unfettered access to the heart of the immortal God, the times and seasons we live in is of course the most appropriate! There's been such pollution as never before in the body of Christ by all manners of strange fires and occultic manipulations that 'appear' like the original. That is why this Worship classic writing by the unassuming and God-loving Minister Javia Denton is most timely and a must-read!

Have you ever wondered why the Prophets will usually require a Minstrel before they are able to prophesy? Have you ever wondered why God is surrounded by the 24 elders casting down their crowns in worship? Have you ever wondered why worship precedes the word ministration in most order of services?

I tell you, the real truth is, without worship, no access! To his heart, nor to his hand!

It is wisdom to explore this worship classic so that you can have a more frequent and unhindered access to the heart of the Father by yourself!

Welcome to heaven on earth through Worship!

Shalom!

REVEREND DAPO ADEGBOYEGA
SENIOR PASTOR/EUROPE CO-ORDINATOR
WORLD EVANGELISM BIBLE CHURCH
INTERNATIONAL HEADQUARTERS
LONDON.

Preface

Dear reader,

I was greatly honoured to be asked to write a preface to this book titled the Worshippers Purpose. I cannot but applaud the depth of knowledge and revelation with which Sister Bunmi Javia Denton writes. She writes as one anointed, inspired and intellectually graced to deal with this subject matter.

For me, this treasure of a book, this worshipper's manual, this self-re-evaluation material comes highly recommended by me to every worshipper.

I particularly love the way she explored the different types of worship, what worship can do, the how to worship, etc.

A wise person once said 'if the use of a thing is not known Abuse is inevitable.' If care is not taken as worship leaders who might have led worship over the years ... one could end up just going through the motions, singing naturally or just skilfully without actually ministering or worshipping in spirit and in truth. As worshippers we need to worship with revelation, we need to dig deeper and not deny ourselves and the congregations we lead of greater experiences and deeper episodes of heavenly downpour we can experience individually and corporately. We need to rekindle the fire of our love to walk with GOD. We need to know that we have an all-seeing audience of ONE who keeps inviting us to come up hither, to dig deeper, to clear our ears and heart of things that hinder us from enjoying and being shown great and mighty things that we know not.

Furthermore, Sister Bunmi shares that 'Our worship should come from a deep understanding of Gods worth which should produce deep respect and appreciation for who He is.' Don't become familiar with GOD, there is so much of HIM to discover that will make you fall helplessly in love with HIM.

'Worship is the very centre of our faith.'

I implore you the reader not to treat this book like another book on worship but one written with depth, with revelation and inspired revelation.

Many times we read books on worship, and you could almost see loads of similarities in the definitions or explanations. This is different, it's fresh, and it comes highly recommended.

Stay blessed.

From a fellow worshipper
Shola Victor-Sajowa

Introduction

It is a pleasure and an honour to finally be able to put this information together.

I am thankful to God for using me as a vessel and an instrument of change in this generation. The purpose of writing this book is to increase awareness regarding worship.

As a contemporary worship leader, over the years, my passion for worship has developed to an insatiable hunger for God's will and purpose regarding my gifting. Carrying this burden for a while has led me to seek for a clearer understanding of God's heart regarding worship.

I wear many 'hats' in life. As a full-time Law lecturer, wife, mother of three children, mentor and worship leader, my lifestyle can be very hectic with a lot of 'distracting' turns. This has been a source of concern to me hence I have decided to action these concerns by carrying out what I call a personal evaluation review. All aspects of my so-called hectic lifestyle have now come under the evaluative, and analytical microscope of purpose and destiny and the big question that emerged from this inquisition is 'are you fulfilled in the midst of the running around?'

I thought I was at least fulfilling part of my purpose due to the fact that I make a great impact in educating hundreds of students and helping them move on to fulfil their dreams in life. I minister in various programs, and people's lives are transformed, I am very selfless and sacrifice a lot to all around me and have written and produced an EP which has again transformed lives (just a few of my personal favourite people centred achievements). However, I was taken aback when in 2013 a friend of mine said I am glad you produced your EP, but I really thought you would write a book! I smiled and asked her why? Her response was well; you have so much to say that makes sense so why not share it with everyone who needs it.

Of course, I buried that under the carpet and excused it away with 'tangible' reasons why no one will want to hear from me when there are other seasoned authors out there in high circles!

I have carried the burden to write this book for a while but have been filled with excuses albeit genuine ones until I had an operation in December 2014 which opened my eyes to the reality of how easily one can pass away without leading a fulfilled life. I realised how simple it is for the unassuming person to go to the grave without fulfilling their assignment on earth. How effortless it is for one to return to dust with a lot of useful gifts and talents that could have helped make your world, or better still the world at large a more bearable or even an enjoyable place for one, two or three fellow humans!

> 'Your revelation(s) could be the resolution(s) to some one's troubled existence but you would never know unless you put it out there!'

It is very simple and is based on the fact that as soon as you are able to figure out your God-ordained mandate and begin to function in it, your life will definitely yield results.

> 'The sad reality is that many do not believe in God's ability to entrust them with such an assignment and even when they do they do not believe in themselves to be able to deliver.'

You must begin by believing in yourself and stop seeking approval from man, you must understand that you will only be relevant and accepted by those that you have been sent to.

> 'Fulfilment of purpose is not dependent on numbers but on impact.'

It is about your ability to use your gifts and talents to empower others or channel others towards understanding their assignment, thriving in their ordained purpose and fulfilling their destinies. A well-spent life is a life offered in service to others wherever you find yourself. You must leave a positive legacy wherever life takes you irrespective of the level you are operating on.

You cannot be the sole solution provider so just be yourself and give your best!

I attended a training session at work, and the question we were asked was 'what would you like to be inscribed on your headstone when you die?' This was the catalyst that got me restless! It opened up something in me that kept me wide-awake spiritually.

During my personal evaluative search, I discovered that I had limited knowledge and a poor understanding, of my purpose and destiny. This was as a result of my limited knowledge and pitiable consideration of God's criteria. Purely because I was content with the 'norm' i.e. attending services and conferences, reading the word and even preaching the word at meetings when invited, writing worship songs inspired by the Holy Spirit, preparing messages and leading people at services or conferences, seminars, etc. I really thought I was on track and ticking the boxes!

Why did I still feel empty deep down inside? Don't get me wrong, I do pray and fast to the best of my ability, I do my best to live right, I also attend seminars and do what most worship leaders are taught to do to develop. However, I remained hungry! And to my surprise the more I searched, the hungrier I became.

I have attended numerous worship services, and in some cases, it has been a case of deja-vu; I see the same practices, patterns and trends occurring. I have seen worship leaders mimicking behaviour patterns, replicating the stereotypes, recycling 'Christianese' phrases, trying to out-sing others, having the wrong focus and I have seen the backup singers do the same and worse.

In some instances, I invite myself to worship events or services, sit in the congregation and observe. In my numerous observations, I have been able to spot the rivalry and contention that is going on in the worship team or that has gone on in the team! In some instances, I have also seen some members of the congregation distracted during worship, busy looking around, and chatting with each other as they become impressed/unimpressed by the whole act/show. I have even seen some people on their phones during worship!

However, I must say irrespective of the minority negative discoveries, to God be the glory there were still some who were deep in worship and my hunger to understand what to do increased! I have come to the conclusion that in order to be satisfied, you have to understand God for yourself (not anyone else). He introduced Himself as the great I am, the God of Abraham, Isaac and Isreal. You have to understand why you believe in Him, why you need Him and who He is. You need to have a clear understanding of your role in the relationship, then and only then can you figure out how to walk with Him and enjoy fellowship with Him.

Therefore, it gives me great pleasure and fulfilment to share with you these Holy Spirit inspired truths which have allowed me to walk with God and worship Him in total freedom.

These truths have also paved the way for my understanding regarding freedom in Him. They have also allowed me to be myself and desist from emulating any trend whatsoever.

These truths have helped me to respond to the beat of heaven's rhythm.

You can only dance in tune with the rhythm if you understand the beat otherwise your dance will be off rhythm and result in confusion.

Today, I keep on developing as I walk daily with the understanding that I am an imperfect being, living in an imperfect world, created to show forth the praises of a perfect God.

Unlike the angels who were created to perfection and live in a perfect heaven; I continually relinquish all I am and pursue the course of being acquainted with this lifestyle that will pleasure my King on a daily basis. Knowing that as long as I keep taking those positive tiny baby steps in the right direction, I am drawing closer to my goal; and even though my hunger for a deeper revelation is still on the increase daily, I am satisfied daily as long as I am with the King.

Please be advised that this book does not distinguish between the terms 'worship' and 'praise' as the focus of this book is to help you understand how to fulfil the mandate given to us at adoption which is to love the Lord with all we are. As a result, I have not concerned myself with frivolous debates regarding the differences between praise and worship. I use the terminology frivolous because God is not interested in how many praise words you offer or how many worship words you offer! In my opinion, these debates produce no beneficial results to my quest for intimacy with God; as a result, I have steered clear of them.

I was sharing some of these truths with a remarkable woman of God and Prophetess Blessing Asanya, a branch Pastor of World Evangelism Bible International Church and visionary of Daughter of Zion Ministry and she told me to put the information in a book so here we are today. Many thanks to her for putting me under immense pressure, she kept going on and on about putting something down in a book. It's amazing what comes out of you when you are squeezed!

The overarching aim of this book is to open your eyes to the 'secrets' or 'truths' hidden in the mystery that is called worship.

> *'that your eyes of understanding being enlightened that ye may know what is the hope of His calling and what the riches of the glory of His inheritance in the saints'*
> *Ephesians 1:18*

Once that has happened, the Holy Spirit in you should help you to truthfully challenge your worship lifestyle, inspire you to change your attitude towards worship and motivate you to worship God alone in spirit and in truth.

A very big thank you to God, who has given me this revelation and allowed me to fulfil my purpose. To my mum, who went back to bible college and has just graduated at the age of 75, you are such an inspiration and a pacesetter. To my husband Peter for allowing me to be me. My awesome children Shanice, Tamara and Tyron who have challenged and inspired me in innumerable ways, and to all the men and women of God who have believed in me and given me a platform in their ministries to express my gifts. To all members of my extended family, friends and loved ones who have encouraged me and believed in me. I pray that the Lord will honour you and reward you all!

All the glory must be to the Lord!

Bunmi Javia Denton
South Ockendon, Essex UK
April 2016

Chapter 1

Man's Mandate

Why Am I Here?

Have you ever reached a point in your journey in life where you questioned why you are here? Have you ever wondered what the point of living or existing was about?

Well, I have.

There are two common passages for all human beings irrespective of your status, gender, beliefs or classification; the entry and the exit routes. We are all born, and we all die; this is a constant.

Whatever happens in between is variable and subject to the diverse classification criteria available in our world systems.

The irony of it all is that we bring nothing on our arrival and we take nothing when we depart.

It is very important to understand this concept as this will inform the choices you make while you are here. Why then should we bother with anything? Why then should we work so hard and accumulate wealth just to leave it all behind? Is it right for a Christian to amass wealth?

The Bible is clear on leaving an inheritance and wealth.

'A good man leaves an inheritance to his children. And the wealth of the sinner is stored up for [the hands of] the righteous.'

Proverbs 13:22

This scripture notifies us that anyone who is good must leave a legacy for their children — biological or otherwise. Your posterity is very important, you should be thinking about the generations coming after you and how you will be remembered. Legacy is not just money and material things which can be devalued or squandered. You could leave a legacy of profitable information, inventions and ideas that will enable the future generations to have a better experience on earth. You can also leave a legacy of a good name and a righteous heritage; you can be that shining example for your posterity to follow.

Be informed that ill-gotten wealth in any family lineage will be squandered, this is what the Bible means. Wealth got by sinful, and treacherous means never result in anything good. It will be transferred for the cause of the righteous. If you do your best to make sure it is passed on to your children, after you are gone it will be transferred! God is not mocked, and He watches over His word to bring it to fulfilment!

Another irony is certain people toil so hard and amount to nothing while some toil very hard and achieve much.

Yet another irony is some do not toil and are born into wealth and high ranking status, go ahead and maintain their wealth while others lose it.

On the other hand, some are born into abject poverty and end up becoming movers and pacesetters while some die worse off than their birth circumstances.

These are some of the reasons why it is important to ask the question regarding your destiny.

'Would it not be awesome if we all had an idea of what we are here for and where we fit into the whole puzzle called life?'

Following my personal quest, I have come to the realisation that man's primary assignment on earth is to worship the Lord and to have fellowship with Him. Every other achievement is inferior and subordinate to this.

This mandate is hidden in the summary of all the commandments.

The commandments were given to man by God to ensure ease in fellowship, to make certain that man knows what to do and what not to do when communing with the creator, to maintain harmony between the two realms. To help man retain a state of virtuous living which will ensure the relationship exists without difficulty and complications.

> 'When man is in good standing with his creator
> blessings are released'

Even the earth stands up as a helper and opens up her mouth to swallow the raging and turbulent flood from the mouth of the serpent our sworn enemy (Revelations 12:15-16). The serpents and the dragons of life will keep on spewing rage from their mouth as this is their purpose however you will always be in a position to bruise their heads if you submit to the plans God has for you; as they are of good and not of evil and they are meant to prosper you and not to harm you, they are for good and not for disaster, they are for your welfare and not for calamity, they are of peace and not for affliction, to give you a good and bright future and establish your hopes until they bring you to your expected end. (Jerimiah 29:11)

All the commandments are summarised in this simple phrase:

> 'To love your God with all your heart, soul, mind and strength.'
> Deuteronomy 6:5, Mark 12:30, Mathew 22:36, Luke 10:27.

In order to attain this mandate, it is very important that man has an understanding of what love is (as explained by God himself) and how to communicate this love to God. If you have ever been in a relationship, you can affirm that love is a two-way street. You can also affirm that love needs to be communicated from the one doing the loving to the one who is being loved and everyone has a unique love language. God explained this to us with the perfect example.

'For God so loved the world that He gave His only begotten son that whosoever believeth in Him will not perish but have everlasting life.'

John 3:16

God's love language is giving.

It is also imperative that we discover for ourselves on an individual basis what God wants from us and how He wants us to love Him.

'Praise the Lord! (Hallelujah!) Blessed [fortunate, prosperous, and favoured by God] is the man who fears the Lord [with awe-inspired reverence and worships Him with obedience], Who delights greatly in His commandments.

His [spiritual] offspring shall be mighty on earth; The generation of the upright shall be blessed.'

Psalm 112: 1-2

This has to be personal because we all are created with diverse strengths and have been given different gifts and talents. We also have personal weaknesses which produce personal challenges. Finally, our lives are presented with different opportunities which can be geographical, economic and even environmental. All these factors have a huge part to play in your orientation and your makeup, but they are not limitations as you have the power to rise above them. Therefore we all need to begin by embarking on a personal quest for enlightenment and knowledge that can bring us to a place where we can understand our assignments, fulfil our purposes and accomplish our divine destinies.

Only this can bring true satisfaction!

Until this happens, it is possible to keep on chasing shadows and leading an unfulfilled life.

'An unfulfilled life is a wasted destiny!'

Money, fame and success are only tools that grant access to opening certain doors in life, but they do not fulfil that deep hunger of accomplishment of assignment, purpose and destiny.

If truly they do then we should not have any (mentally stable) rich person commit suicide as a result of being dissatisfied with their life. We should not have the rich chasing after more money, the famous pursuing more fame and the 'successful' hunting down more success. Don't get me wrong money and fame could make life very comfortable but they do not always totally satisfy.

We must get to a place in life where we are of the understanding that we may never be satisfied in life until we see our Saviour, but we should not live a life of starvation, constantly craving what we cannot have and never appreciative of the things that we are in possession of.

We must get to a point where we can say

> 'I am no longer starving because I understand my assignment, and every day, I am in pursuit of my purpose, therefore, I am fulfilling my destiny irrespective of how much I have and who I know. As long as I am making an impact and fulfilling God's will for me, I am fine.'

It is not easy or quick to get to this place of reason, but it is possible.

In order to get to this place of cognitivism, you will need to do a lot of stripping. It takes a lot of stripping of oneself of many theories that have been indoctrinated to you knowingly or unknowingly by your environment, life experiences, conditioning and orientation.

You would have to strip yourself of every layer that does not add substantial value to you. You must strip off every layer that causes you pain and challenges your self-worth and esteem, every layer that causes you to feel uncomfortable with who you are and causes you to crave validation from man rather than from God. Every layer that makes you operate under peer pressure as well as unhealthy and unnecessary competition which leaves only one loser — you!

You will have to strip yourself down to the bone and then allow God to build you up.

You are the only one who can identify those poisonous and contaminated layers that only keep you sick in the spirit, wear you out and choke your destiny.

Once you have identified them, you must strip yourself of them.

It could be your so called friends, your bad habits and secret addictions, pride, selfishness, lack of education, bad attitude, laziness, insecurities, etc. It could be extremely painful to part with them because they have been grafted deep into you that you have even believed that is who you are! You must remember that if you don't get rid of them they will keep on overshadowing and truncate your purpose and you will not fulfil your mandate.

You must also understand that this is a process, if you pick off an unripe fruit, (e.g. banana, mango or any fruit that should be enjoyed when it is ripe), you will end up with a sour version and never get to experience how pleasant it can taste. However, if you wait till the process nature has for it is fulfilled then you will be in a position to appreciate the fruit.

Processing is vital, just as one can never eat all the food and drink all the water one needs for survival throughout one's lifetime in one instant. Rather one can and should only eat and drink to satisfy the hunger and thirst of that particular moment as it will be enough to take you through to the next feeding time, so we should be in our pursuit of God's purpose and mandate regarding our lives.

We should not be parched, starving or malnourished regarding what we need to fulfil our assignment, purpose or our destinies but we should be fed and watered and keep on being in-filled throughout our daily individual journeys.

In order to do this you as an individual need to stop comparing and contrasting your assignment, purpose, mandate and destiny to other's around you but focus on our own individual walk with God.

What Are the Rules to Understanding My Mandate?

There are always terms and conditions in life, and if they are not adhered to, you will always get an adverse result.

As a human being, if you do not begin your day with the basic essential routines you will end up losing out in one area or the other, it is irrelevant if you are aware of what the routines are or not.

For example, if you are attending an interview, meeting a friend for coffee or even taking your baby to the local toddler group and you have not taken the time to clean your teeth, wash, put on clean clothing and remember to adhere to certain behavioural codes, you will encounter obstacles throughout your journey.

Even though there is no rulebook listing these terms and conditions, it is expected of you as a regular human being to have an understanding of how your body works and the expectations of the society you live in. You are expected to understand that if you do not wash you will smell, you cannot go out naked and many basic rules that govern society.

Even if you had the opportunity to be born and raised in a palace, you would notice that your breath, appearance, emotions, etc. change when you change certain things about them like all other human beings, not of noble birth. So if you showed up to the interview/meeting/toddler group smelling, dirty and unkempt, it will be apparent to others that something is not right and you would be a cause for concern even if you do not know it. Especially if the people you are meeting are of the understanding that you are mentally sound!

You are just like any invention, and you come with a guidebook, if you are not assembled and used in accordance with your specific guidebook, the outcome will be unfavourable. Therefore you must study and understand the guidebook of you before assembly and usage even by yourself.

You must also understand that initial assembly or usage can occur on your behalf as we are all subject to influence from parents, guardians, schools, friends and many other geographical, environmental and circumstantial factors; before we are able to take charge of our destinies. However, once your eyes are open to your ability and capability to take charge of your destiny, then you are without excuse and the whole of creation is awaiting your manifestation as a son of God! (Romans 1: 8)

This is a tough decision to make as it is very difficult to change even though the only constant in life is change!

Many great and wholesome people today, have taken out time to evaluate and restructure their destinies to align with God's will and purpose for their lives.

Whatever you do after reading this book, please do not remain at the point where you assume you know what you are doing, with the product called your life and attempt to set it up only to end up frustrated due to not achieving the anticipated results. Instead, spend more time going back to the guidebook so you can get the anticipated results!

The guidebook is a combination of the book of life (Bible) and your own spiritual DNA.

'Your spiritual DNA is made out of your strengths, gifts, talents and capabilities, weaknesses, in capabilities, opportunities and all those unique things that make you who you are!'

Chapter 2
Worship Defined

I begin by exploring the definition(s) of the word Worship. As it is important to shed some light on this mystery that makes our creator so content with us when we get it right.

In the Bible, you will find a wide variety of words utilised to describe or explain the word worship.

In the midst of these synonyms are some precise Hebrew words, some specific Greek words and other words in both languages that have a meaning depicting the word Worship.

English Definition

The English definition of the word worship is to offer reverent admiration, to formally or ceremoniously render honour, to express profound adoration, devotion and respect and pay homage to God. The word worship is a verb (an action word).

You as an individual will have to find a way bearing in mind your spiritual DNA of meeting these criteria, there are many places of worship that provide you with an opportunity to meet with others however from the above definition it is clear that this is an action that cannot be done on your behalf.

Only you can offer your worship.

Just as I cannot admire your spouse for you, I cannot express your profound adoration for your spouse for you in ways that only you can, I cannot be devoted to your marriage or respect your relationship for you, the same way I cannot offer worship for you or vice versa.

You are the only one who can feel what you feel. You can ask me to help you put your feelings into words or create the perfect environment or write the perfect speech for you. I can only replicate what you describe based on my understanding of your ideas, but I cannot feel what you feel for your spouse.

In the same manner, you are the only one who can feel admiration and reverence for God in a certain way and then go ahead and perform the feeling as an act of worship. This explains why when you are in a meeting people respond to worship differently.

> 'Your response is dependent on the depth of your understanding of who God is and your appreciation of the role He plays in your life.'

This is then translated into your act of worship.

If you have the understanding that God does not reside in a physical place of worship, then you will recognise why you do not have to rely on being in a building or being with anyone to feel and express your worship to God.

If you have the understanding that He has decided to reside in your heart to ensure it is possible for you to live, move and have your being in Him; it will be natural or second nature for you to reach deep down and express profound admiration to the king who deserves it wherever you are and irrespective of what is going on.

Furthermore, if you have the understanding that He sits in anticipation of what you will bring to Him, you will gladly go ahead and offer your worship from your heart.

You may need coaching to learn how to connect with your feelings. Although this is a natural trait, some people have been disconnected or have disconnected themselves with their emotional side. You will need to get back in touch with your feelings in order to worship as worship requires you to commune with your maker with a grateful heart.

Hebrew Definitions

Since the Bible was written in Hebrew, it is really important to understand the intended meaning of words used. As a multilingual person (I speak more than one language and studied other languages as well as my first degree), I am aware that a word could have multiple meanings depending on the context in which it is used. Even English words have synonyms, and the intended meaning of a word will dictate the choice of synonym used. It is therefore very important to understand the original language and meanings of the words used, so we get a true picture as meanings get lost in translations.

There are a few Hebrew words used synonymously in the Bible to represent the word Worship. Below are five Hebrew words used and their tangible translations:

1) Shachah (Original word הַחָוֹשׁ, pronounced shaw-khaw)

The literal meaning of this word is to physically depress or prostrate yourself. The following English synonyms are used in the Bible: fall down, crouch, humbly beseech, and make to stoop. The worship is used 100 times, the phrase bow-down 54 times, the phrase do obeisance 9 times, the phrase do reverence 5 times.

Why Shachah?

Many questions came to my mind when I tried to understand this word.

For example 'what if the person is physically challenged due to a disability and cannot accomplish this position, does this mean they are unable to fulfil this criterion?'

'Should we all physically prostrate or crouch in church?'

I came to the conclusion that the requirement in this state is an attitude because you could lie prostrate on the floor in worship, but your heart or lifestyle is standing tall in defiance to God!

You are allowed to physically depress yourself in church or in your private closet however God is seeking for a state of humility! Remember it's not about how man perceives you. You may appear humble on the outside but what are you truly like on the inside?

This specific word with a wide variety of meanings was chosen deliberately by the Holy Spirit who inspired the Hebrew writer because of God's desire and not to get approval from man.

> 'Once you start seeking for approval from man you have missed the mark!'

Human beings are very unstable, and their fluid standards change in response to motive, environment, anticipated results and many more targets however God's standards never change.

Make sure you choose God's standard

> 'For no matter how many promises God has made, they are 'Yes in Christ. And so through him the 'Amen' is spoken by us to the glory of God'
>
> *2 Corinthians 1:20 NIV*

2) Abad (Original word עָבַד pronounced aw-bad)

This word when translated means to serve, to be enslaved. This word is used more than 250 times in the Old Testament, and 31 times with the word shachah.

Why Abad?

We need to remember that the Old Testament was set in the era where slavery was an acceptable social behaviour. Times have changed, and presently there is legislation that frown on such behaviour. Personally, my interpretation of this word is again another attitude of complete loyalty in response to the creator-creature relationship. The only knowledge I have about slavery is what I had acquired from books, films and other information sources as this was way before my existence and my ancestry was not positioned in a location where they were taken and enslaved so I have no generational history or accounts passed down.

Even though I do not have any first-hand experience of slavery, I am of the knowledge that as a slave you lived out your master's will, you had no control over your life, will, purpose or destiny because your whole existence was to serve your master whether you liked it or not!

Your master provided you with an assignment based on his opinion of your ability and capability and expected you to complete it within a stipulated target period. Whether it was convenient or not for you, whether you understood it or not and you faced punitive consequences for your failure to achieve irrespective of all the explanations we can find! You could be priced possession or a replaceable waste of space depending on whose hands you ended up in!

Thankfully we do not serve a God who is irrational or who is ignorant of our abilities and capabilities as the slave masters were. We serve a God who is the master of our destinies, and we are His masterpieces individually created by Him. He fully understands us, knows our expiry dates and is able to shorten or extend it because He hears prayers and sees tears (Isaiah 38:1-8)

He is not cruel either; in fact, one of His attributes is that He is abundant in mercy and full of compassion!

David asked God to blot out his transgressions and show some mercy out of the multitude of tender mercies God possesses! (Psalm 51)

So why did the writer use this word to illustrate what God wants from us?

This word choice gives me an insight into the state of mind we should have as worshippers.

This also explains the reason why worship cannot only happen in the church building, or before your prayer meeting or any of the stereotypes that we have been led to believe and practice! In those days, if you were a slave you remained a slave in your sleep or when you are awake performing for your master's wishes. You remained a slave until you were redeemed and given your freedom.

Therefore, if we are to worship the Lord our God and serve Him only (Luke 4:8). Then it should encompass every aspect of our lives irrespective of if we are in a church building, conference, house fellowship, dinner party, wedding, gym, kitchen ……I am sure you get my drift!

We are reminded that whatever we do, we should work at it with all our hearts as working for the Lord and not as working for human beings. (Colossians 3:23)

3) Darash (Original word: שָׁרַשׁ pronounced daw-rash)

This word means to seek. Some of my preferred English synonyms for the word seek include: to pursue, try and find, hunt for, seek out and strive to have. As you can see, they are all proactive words and denote the need for action. Seeking is not a passive word or state of mind, I dare to suggest it is a continuum and you can only stop when you go back to be with the Lord.

Why Darash?

I believe you seek with your heart first. Your brain must recognise the need and then translate the message to your eyes. In fact, I don't know if you have ever misplaced or lost something valuable and you begin to seek for or strive to find. Your emotions will go all over the place depending on the value of what you lost, your heart will race; you will pace about and turn everywhere upside down trying to find it. You may even employ the help of others if they are available. Indeed I am sure it is fair to say your whole peace for the day or moment would be disrupted until you find it.

You will only find your peace again, be settled and relieved when you find it. If you do not find it, this might even cause you to shed a tear or two or be angry and frustrated. In fact, this emotional turbulence may exceed a day depending on the value of what you lost and the circumstances of the loss. A classic example is a mother who loses her child for a moment at a superstore, she will know no peace until that child has been handed back to her.

Seeking is born out of hope and determination.

Hope begins with a desire, which is then seen as attainable.

This is what propels one to carry on.

The hope of finding what you are looking for and the determination to keep on going until you find it!

Hope is a continuum, you decide when you give up but as long as you hope you cannot be ashamed (Romans 5:5).

> 'The greatest irony of the matter to me personally is we seek, yet Christ is in us, and He is the hope of glory!'

How amazing that a God is so great for the heavens to contain and who uses the whole earth as His footstool decides to set up His dwelling place in the heart of Man!

This really is a mystery because how can we be expected to seek for what is in us and still struggle to find it?

It is written that when we become born again, we are new creatures, Christ is meant to move in and take over. His nature should create in you a new man, that inner man which cannot be bought with money or come into existence as a result of any religious practice, not as a result of rituals or rites, and it cannot even be attained by the laying of hands! It cannot be transferred or inherited.

It can only be attained when you surrender your life to Christ and allow your life to be joined or grafted to the Lord Jesus Christ and allow His Spirit to live in you.

'He must be in the driving seat always, not seasonally or when you are in a crisis! He cannot be manipulated or deceived.'

The result of this is the death of your former man/spirit, and the birth of light and glory manifested in the obvious power of God to all and sundry.

You must die to pride, lust, unhealthy competition, selfish ambition, anger, wrath, sexual immorality, idolatry, the love and enslavement to mammon, theft, lies, hypocrisy, deceit and all those layers that hinder you from achieving your mandate.

When this is attained and only then can you find what you are seeking for.

Hope is found in redemption, there is hope for us all in God; our hope is an anchor of the soul which is steadfast and not uncertain.

He invites us to seek and assures us that we will find (Mathew 7:7).

He also assures us that He is with us always even unto the end of the age. Therefore, our part is to seek to recognise His presence not by goosebumps or any physical or emotional means but by cultivating the ability to discern good and evil, and we keep on evolving from glory to glory; we in Christ and Christ in us; it goes hand in hand not one without the other.

The testimony of our search must be this: in Him we live and move and have our being (Acts 17:28)

4) Yare (Original Word: יָרֵא pronounced yaw-ray)

Yare means to fear.

Fear exists in many degrees; I have experienced fear for many reasons and in some of the many degrees that fear exists.

If you have been around toddlers, you will understand me when I say we are born fearless. They have no concept of fear! They keep on going to that place that makes you jump or keep putting everything in their mouths as they have no concept of fear.

They even think it is funny to run off into the road!

However unfortunately or fortunately we all get introduced to fear from a young age, and it ends up being a silent and sometimes secret life companion.

Some of us had fear invited and given a comfortable abode into our lives by our parents! While some of us experienced fear as a result of an unfortunate incident that happened to us directly or to other we know or do not know. The circumstances of your acquaintance with fear is irrelevant; the truth of the matter is you will know or recognise fear when you have an encounter with it. It is a unique emotion that can trigger extreme ends of behaviour. You can either freeze or take to your heels, shout or remain silent. Some people have even been known to wet or defecate themselves as a result of this emotion, some lie, exaggerate or completely forget what they are trying to say. Fear leave its mark whenever if visits.

However, the secret is only the perfect love of God can cast fear out (1John 4:18).

> 'You will only know if fear is still with you when you face challenges. You can be so accommodating and acquainted to fear so much that you are able to live with it, feed it, nurture it, love it, hate it, mask it, express it, excuse it in various ways albeit legitimate and even be controlled by it!'

I am a very optimistic person, and I believe I have mastered a few emotions, or I am on the learning curve however fear reminded me of its power and influence recently. It also reminded me of the constant need to review my state of affairs because I may be deluded believing I have mastered fear.

The truth is every time you forget the depth and breadth of the love God has for you, fear will wangle its way back in and once you depend on the truth of God's love it will have no choice but to disappear!

I discovered that I was afraid when I had to undergo surgery 2 years ago. It hit me just before I was overtaken by the anaesthetic substance administered. I felt a wide range of emotions and thoughts rush through my being, I even decided not to inhale the gas until I was sure I had made my peace with God within me just in case I did not wake back up. Nobody knew this was going on because I had my fear hiding mask on and was masking my fear of dying and leaving my children at a young age.

I did not remember that I have been promised long life and salvation (Psalm 91:16)!

The theatre staff who prepared me for the procedure were lovely and engaged me in conversation, they were busy trying to distract me and prepare me emotionally for the procedure but I was a masked mess deep inside, and nobody could see it!

Why Yare?

Is God's word controversial? Why does He expect us to fear Him then inform us that He has not given us a spirit of fear? How can He tell us He is love and perfect love drives away fear and then expect us to Yare in worship? These again are some of my personal queries.

I then came to the realisation that the kind of fear we need to have for God in worship is a deep reverential fear because He is the master of the universe and has the power and authority over all! Not the dark fear we have when in doubt of God's ability to come through for us.

Does this mean we should approach God with the fear of punishment?

Some people have a fire insurance policy with God; the fear of going to hell!

Undoubtedly vengeance belongs to Him, however, most importantly the kind of fear we should have for Him is a Holy fear coming from a place of respect and admiration with an understanding of how much it cost Him to redeem you and me.

> 'The worth you place on the relationship you have or desire to have with the father and the cost of losing it would determine the kind of fear that should be upon you when you approach Him in worship.'

5) Avah (Original Word: הָוָא pronounced aw-vaw)

This word means to crave.

I have physical cravings and emotional craving. However, the worst and weirdest recurrent cravings I have ever had was in childbirth. I craved ice cubes! So a few weeks to my due date I fill the freezer with ice which comes with me to the hospital. During labour, I spend every interval I get from crying due to the pain or dozing off from the gas and air crunching on ice until I birth my babies!

If you have ever had a craving, you would understand the fact that cravings could end up driving you up the wall until they are satisfied. They become an obsession as they occupy your every thought until they are fulfilled.

For addicts, their cravings cannot be controlled as these cravings occupy a priority spot in their thoughts and take over their whole existence.

Why Avah?

God needs us to have a deep craving for Him, we need to hunger after Him in worship with an understanding that He is our satisfaction and without Him, we can never be fulfilled.

Simply put we need to be addicted to God, we should seek to walk with Him, talk with Him, exchange our will for His and be overcome by Him.

We need to long for Him with such hunger that only He alone can resolve! If you find satisfaction elsewhere, you might have an idol...

Greek Definitions

There are also a few Greek words used synonymously in the Bible to represent the word Worship. Below are three of the words used and their translations:

1) Proskuneo

This means to kiss like a dog licking his master's hand, to kiss the ground before a king or to kiss the feet of a king and this is used 59 times in the Bible.

Why Proskuneo?

My imagination of why a person will want to respond to another person in this manner is full of pictures that depict the one doing the kissing as being in possession of an excessive degree of admiration, awe, respect and affection. This can be the only reason why anyone will willingly desire to respond to another person in this manner especially when they are not obliged to do so!

This is again an attitude as we cannot physically see God, never mind grabbing His feet and kissing them!

This attitude is also accompanied by the need to please the recipient and can only develop as a result of the amount of love and affection that you hold in your heart regarding the receptor of your kisses.

God is a worthy God!

He is even worthy of your kisses and affection which gets rejected by man!

> 'Stop wasting your affection on people and things that do not deserve it instead channel them to the lover of your soul!'

He deserves to be showered with our affection and love.

True affection cannot be forced, it can be faked to impress onlookers or the recipient, however, the giver of fake affection is always aware that they are living a lie and they are always under the burden to keep it going.

On the other hand, true affection flows easily from the giver, and it is the best gift.

The giver enjoys offering it, and the receiver enjoys accepting it.

You cannot fake affection towards God as he is omniscient.

It is a pointless act as there is only one loser — the faker!

Anyone who has a dog(s) will tell you that they will only respond to you with numerous lickings of your hand, face, etc. as a result of forming a rapport with you which has resulted in them developing a sense of security and ease around you especially if you are not their owner.

If not they will bark and try to inform you of their insecurities and their readiness to attack you or defend themselves from you if they find your closeness threatening.

If an animal has the ability to recognise the need to show appreciation or the need to communicate its response to the love of its keeper or anyone they have bonded with. If it is aware that it needs to respond to the love that has been or is being shown. If this comes naturally to animals, then it should be our nature to respond to our maker and master in a manner that shows our acknowledgement of His love, redemption, care, protection, faithfulness, mercy, provision, direction, divine intervention, grace and participation in all aspects of our lives and circumstances.

2) Sebomai

This means to reverence or to hold in awe, and this particular word is used 10 times in the Bible.

Why Sebomai?

When you reverence or hold something or someone in awe, it is obvious to anyone around you. You will speak about it with respect, you will guard and cherish it, and you will explain why you believe it deserves that type of status in your world.

With some people, it is their favourite singer, football club, parent, child, career, president, entrepreneur, guru, fashion or trend, etc. all you need to do is spend a day with them, and it will be evident to you what they reverence.

'We are to reverence God alone; nothing or no one should take pre-eminence over Him!'

Everything should be secondary, and God should be primary in our lives.

He is Jehovah Elohim, El-Elyon, the sovereign God who created the whole universe with the words of His mouth, angels bow down before Him, there is indeed no one like our God. Lord of all the earth, Alpha Omega, YHWH!

Reverence Him in your worship lifestyle today and kick out all your idols!

3) Latreuo

This means to render religious service of homage. This also is a physical requirement that involves your senses and a conscious decision to yield them completely to the glory of God. It is used 21 times in the New Testament.

Why Latreuo?

It is the full package which is a combination of all the points discussed above including you doing performing a physical service to advance the work of God.

Just going to church is not enough physical service. The Bible talks about a bountiful harvest but few workers. Find a way of making meaningful and consistent contributions to advancing the work of the kingdom in your local church or community.

Whatever you do ensure your service is acceptable in the eyes of God and not for vain glory. Engage your time, talents, gifts and money to the advancement of the kingdom of God.

'Being religious is not enough if there is no relationship.'

Going to church should not be an avenue to compete, show off your new materialistic possessions, gossip, trade, condemn and judge people, intimidate or form cliques that segregate people who are not in your social status, criticise the pastor, quarrel with people who refuse to bow to your will ... I am sure you get my drift!

Participate in worship in a sensitive manner; worship time is not when you entertain all manners of distractions into your life.

In church, it is definitely not the time to catch up with social media, scan the congregation for the latest fashion sense, see who is sitting where, manipulate people and do all those things that rob you of having a successful time with the Lord!

Remember our works will be tried by fire! Remember naked we came and so shall we return! Your treasure must be in heaven!

Chapter 3

The Power of Worship

I am sure you are beginning to get some (or more) revelation of what worship is all about! As I keep writing these words, I am also a blessing to myself. I am enjoying and learning from the revelation and inspiration being given by the Holy Spirit.

The above has provided me with the need to reflect and re-evaluate my own worship lifestyle! All the Bible passages used below are quoted from the Amplified Bible due to its self-explanatory style.

As believers, we are introduced to worship.

> *'For you shall not worship any other god; for the LORD, whose name is Jealous, is a jealous (impassioned) God [demanding what is rightfully and uniquely His].'*
>
> *Exodus 34:14*

This is a direct instruction given to all believers.

God is aware of our ability to create and worship idols especially in our hearts. As imperfect beings, we have been instructed to channel that aspect of our emotion to Him alone. In the place of worship, you need to train your mind from wondering about as a lion tamer is able to train a lion to do tricks! It is with the mind that we serve the Lord. The battle of the mind is intense, you must not be ignorant to this; this awareness must be with you at all times and would help keep your mind in check when in the attitude or atmosphere of worship.

In the book of Revelations, we are given an insight of how the perfect beings who live in a perfect world worship. They worship in unison, in spirit and in truth. It is the sound of corporate worship designed for the audience of one. They understand what they are doing and who it is for. They are in one accord and present one sound. No gimmicks, no drama; just one acceptable sound!

Then I heard something like the shout of a vast multitude, and like the boom of many pounding waves, and like the roar of mighty peals of thunder, saying, 'Hallelujah! For the Lord our God, the Almighty, [the Omnipotent, the Ruler of all] reigns!

Revelations 19:6

What Shall I Render? The Correct Attitude to Worship

Since worship involves giving, we must understand that it could be accepted or rejected. With this in mind, we are encouraged to adopt the correct attitude to worship.

'O come, let us worship and bow down, Let us kneel before the LORD our Maker [in reverent praise and prayer]'

Psalm 95:6

If we are before the omniscient, we need to be aware that He sees deep into us and deep into our worship. Therefore if the purpose of your worship to Him is to tick the prayer structure box and get to making selfish requests, He sees! We must come before Him in reverence even though we are free in Him, we must approach Him in recognition of His might

We must always remember that God should be the centre of our worship when we kneel in reverent praise and prayer, not us; irrespective of what you are going through or how tempting it is to be religious or self-centred. God is already aware of your future and the outcome. So, always remember that there is a time to ask for what you need, and you will definitely receive because He promised, a time to knock on doors and they will be opened again because He has promised and a time to seek Him, and you would find Him because He has promised.

'God is a God of principles, and you cannot rearrange His divine plan or order!'

Solomon worshipped in a way no one had ever done. He decided in his heart to bring a unique sacrifice which pleased God. He dedicated his worship to God. His worship was God focused, it was not about Solomon at all, he simply wanted to touch God like no one had and his worship brought Him a divine visitation which was loaded with every solution he needed for his reign as king and for his personal rest.

His destiny and purpose were settled through his worship.

Solomon was the only one who got that turnaround on that day in the midst of the multitude that showed up for the temple rededication service!

Solomon was the first partaker of the blessing because he had no hidden agenda when he worshipped.

I have visited so many services and have witnessed pastors or guest speakers coming in after the praise and worship session. I have also witnessed them remain in a separate room during worship and join only when they are ready to share the word. Personally, I believe this is an error because if you study the original Old Testament worship blueprint, you will notice that the priests were involved in the worship. They did not isolate themselves from the general worship time. There is no need to over-spiritualise things. Your extra preparation should have been done at home before the worship time. As the leader of the flock, you should be there carrying everyone along, participating and partaking of the blessing just like Solomon did.

Jesus Christ offered himself as the ultimate worship sacrifice hence he remains the main focus of the worship offering.

He could have sacrificed one of his disciples or nominated one of the angels to take His place! No amount of 'spirituality' will make God change his word.

King Solomon did not detach himself from the worship service; in fact, he did the opposite as he was the chief participant which resulted in him being the chief beneficiary! (1Kings 3).

During worship, your attitude should be dictated by the question 'what shall I render unto the Lord?' It should never be centred around 'what can the singers or choir render unto the Lord?'

Paul adjures us by the mercies of God to present ourselves a living sacrifice (Romans 12:1).

Therefore only you can fulfil this criterion; this criterion seems to be a continuum meaning as long as you are living, alive and have your being, your life should be and remain a sacrifice unto your Creator.

The only time acceptable to stop presenting yourself as a sacrifice should be when your life comes to an end, and you stop living, breathing and are certified dead.

The prerequisite for this criterion is not based on what happens to you while you are alive; there is no mention of age, seasons, financial circumstances, education, position in the church, or any other imaginable reason. It does not even depend on your religion or belief system. The instruction is for those who are alive.

This is the difference between prayer and worship.

We are equally instructed to pray without ceasing however our prayers are as a result of our needs, state of minds, challenges, etc. therefore prayer is still a receivers game as you are asking for things and not giving back. Don't get me wrong, prayer is very relevant and should remain so.

In the Old Testament, the altar of incense stood before the holy of holies and only the priest could stand there to offer the morning and evening sacrifice. Our prayers go before the Lord as incense.

'Let my prayer be counted as incense before You; The lifting up of my hands as the evening offering.'

Psalm 141:2

'And the smoke and fragrant aroma of the incense, with the prayers of the saints (God's people), ascended before God from the angel's hand.'

Revelation 8:4

Even the four living creatures that present the prayers of the saints before the throne mix it with fresh, pure unadulterated worship.

So if you are going to lead any prayer session, you must partake in the worship session because worship is for Him alone!

'And when He had taken the scroll, the four living creatures and the twenty-four elders fell down before the Lamb (Christ), each one holding a harp and golden bowls full of fragrant incense, which are the prayers of the saints (God's people)

⁹ And they sang a new song [of glorious redemption], saying, 'Worthy and deserving are You to take the scroll and to break its seals; for You were slain (sacrificed), and with Your blood, You purchased people for God from every tribe and language and people and nation. ¹⁰ 'You have made them to be a king-dom [of royal subjects] and priests to our God; and they will reign on the earth.

¹¹ Then I looked, and I heard the voice of many angels around the throne and [the voice] of the living creatures and the elders; and they numbered myriads of myriads, and thousands of thousands (innumerable), ¹² saying in a loud voice, 'Worthy and deserving is the Lamb that was sacrificed to receive power and riches and wisdom and might and honour and glory and blessing.

¹³ And I heard every created thing that is in heaven or on earth or under the earth [in Hades, the realm of the dead] or on the sea, and everything that is in them, saying [together], 'To Him who sits on the throne, and to the Lamb (Christ), be blessing and honour and glory and dominion forever and ever.

¹⁴ And the four living creatures kept saying, 'Amen.' And the el-ders fell down and worshipped [Him who lives forever and ever]'

Revelation 5:8-14

The Bible also is clear about when we should worship.

It has to be interwoven into the fabrics of our daily living. We must live a life of gratitude which will trigger worship. It should be our lifestyle.

'Let us at all times offer up to God a sacrifice of praise, which is the fruit of lips that thankfully acknowledge and confess and glorify His name.'

Hebrews 13:15

We need to let our father know at all times that we are thankful and we acknowledge His awesome power. We need to always glorify His name even if it costs us. A sacrifice must cost you something. If it costs you nothing, it is not a sacrifice.

Worship in Understanding

Our worship must come from a place of understanding of who God is, who we are and the mercy we have received from God; this is the reason for our redemption as explained to us.

'But you are A CHOSEN RACE, A royal PRIESTHOOD, A CON-SECRATED NATION, A [special] PEOPLE FOR God's OWN POSSESSION, so that you may proclaim the excellencies [the wonderful deeds and virtues and perfections] of Him who called you out of darkness into His marvellous light. 10 Once you were NOT A PEOPLE [at all], but now you are GOD'S PEO-PLE; once you had NOT RECEIVED MERCY, but now you have RECEIVED MERCY.'

1Peter 2:9

We need to worship in complete understanding of the cost of redemption. We need to have a full understanding of God's accomplished work concerning our destinies and the price He paid.

We need to be clear that He did not just wave a magic wand which mysteriously resulted in our redemption.

We need to appreciate the planning and execution of redemption's story.

We need to comprehend the privileges of this royal adoption.

We also need to be able to read between the lines and recognise that we have received so much mercy, love and forgiveness. We have been adopted into royalty, we have been given the best gift that no amount of money can or ever will be able to buy. However, we have a part to play, as there is a clause in verse 9:

> 'so that you may proclaim the excellencies [the wonderful deeds and virtues and perfections] of Him who called you out of darkness into His marvellous light.'

We need to understand that the part we have to play is to worship Him!

Most importantly we must worship in joy irrespective of what is going on in our lives at the particular time, having the assurance that God is with us all the time and most importantly He is aware of our pain and is ready to help if you trust Him and allow him to do so.

We are invited to have a positive attitude.

> 'Serve the LORD with gladness and delight; Come before His presence with joyful singing.'
>
> Psalm 100:2

Our spiritual service is to offer acceptable worship to God.

> 'Therefore I urge you, brothers and sisters, by the mercies of God, to present your bodies [dedicating all of yourselves, set apart] as a living sacrifice, holy and well-pleasing to God, which is your rational (logical, intelligent) act of worship.'
>
> Romans 12:1

Because we live in a 'house' which is our body, we cannot worship in absentia of the body. We must ensure our bodies are dedicated and set apart for God. We must lead a holy lifestyle void of pollution and the contamination of sin. Our bodies are meant to be set apart for worship not used as instruments of hedonistic acts. You must set aside self-gratification that is in conflict with God's word. The Bible describes this as a sensible, coherent and intellectual act of worship. If you claim to have any iota of intelligence in you, then you should be able to figure out that your satisfactory act of worship is when your body is kept holy and acceptable to God.

> 'The knowledge of who we are, what we have received and the potency of our creator; should incite us to approach the throne in reverence and awe.'

> *'Therefore, since we receive a kingdom which cannot be shaken, let us show gratitude, and offer to God pleasing service and acceptable worship with reverence and awe.'*
> *Hebrews 12:28*

The kingdom of God is unshakeable, it was established even before time began and will continue in eternity. It is not a fad, it has outlived tales, ages, cultures, religions, sects, ideologies and criticisms. There is evidence of a creator and evidence of who Jesus was when He walked the streets of the earth. There is evidence of His birth, His works, His death and His resurrection. Miracles still happen. God lives and reigns forever, and His kingdom shall never end!

> 'We need to show gratitude and offer to God a worship that is pleasing and acceptable to Him. This is the biblical requirement for worship.'

We are heirs of a solid kingdom, not one that is moved or shaken by time. Many great kingdoms, empires and rules have existed in the past nevertheless they have been shaken, and their authority has been usurped due to their shakeable nature. Our king is the ancient of days and the great I am who was, who is and who is to come!

The service due to this great God must be one that pleases Him.

What He takes pleasure in is our acceptable worship.

He is pleased to know that we are grateful for His awesome gift.

The kind of worship that pleases Him is one offered in reverence and awe!

I can never claim to be the expert however I am persuaded that some of God's expectation for our worship is expressed in the criteria above.

Our worship should reflect an understanding as well as a personal interpretation and application of the definitions discussed earlier in this book which can also be seen in the above scripture.

It should not be what is done in the midst of people singing and playing instruments only but should be a lifestyle that portrays your understanding of the above scripture.

Your worship should come from a deep understanding of God's worth which should produce deep respect and appreciation of who He is!

I am also persuaded that any 'act of worship' performed outside this revelation is empty.

Worship Is an Act of Giving

Your worship should be your way of giving back to God as a result of your understanding and appreciating the love you have received, the forgiveness and mercy you received from the greatest miracle which is salvation.

'Worship is the very centre of faith!'

'But without faith it is impossible to [walk with God and] please Him, for whoever comes [near] to God must [necessarily] believe that God exists and that He rewards those who [earnestly and diligently] seek Him.'

Hebrews 11:6

To believe that God exists is a necessity for your walk with Him.

You cannot walk with God, or even please Him without an assured conviction regarding His existence. You cannot get any understanding or wisdom from Him, never experience His unmerited favour or hear His voice. You can never see His face or lean on the many breasted ones, you can never hide in his secret place or ride on His wings of love, you can never experience unadulterated love and complete rest, you can never know true peace or live a fulfilled life. You can never fully understand your assignment or mandate, never accomplish your purpose or fulfil your destiny unless you come close to Him and receive instructions in worship.

You can never please Him or ever hear Him say well done at the end of your journey if you do not believe that you can find Him in worship.

It all begins in worship and ends in worship. It is important to understand that life in eternity is for worship. We will not even be in this form, and our earthly needs have no place in eternity.

God understands that worship is a sacrifice and He will reward you when sincerely and persistently seek Him. Seeking Him earnestly and diligently is a journey and not a one off. It is a journey that will be loaded with tests, trials, twists and turns. It is written that Jesus went to the wilderness to fast and pray for 40 days and when He came out He was confronted by Satan, and He had to resist the enemy. Jesus had to be mature, earnest and diligent in His walk. I would have expected that the miracles should have just been oozing out of Jesus due to the amount of fasting, prayer and isolation time He had invested in His walk with the Lord. Instead, Jesus was confronted with trials and temptation, and the miraculous began after he had mastered the trials and temptations by resisting Satan.

It takes maturity (consistent development) to be diligent in the place of worship especially in a world full of distractions. It takes a lot of character and strength to build up maturity, and it takes a lot of overcoming of adversity to build up character. Not only then can you resist and overcome the enemy. You can never and should never expect a smooth ride in your walk with God. However, you must always expect victory at the end of every challenge. This is the reason for the reward!

'But the people who [are spiritually mature and] know their God will display strength and take action [to resist].'

Daniel 11:32

'We have not seen Jehovah but believe He exists; this is the height of our faith, therefore, worshipping Him whom we have not seen but believe is the omnipotent creator and ruler of all, is the pinnacle of faith!'

We can only come near to Him, walk with Him and please Him by faith.

We can only get the assurance by faith that prayers rendered earnestly and diligently are answered, and good deeds are rewarded by Him.

You need to understand that you can display strength and take action to resist the mutual enemy (Satan) whose sole aim is to kill, steal and destroy (your ordained assignment, purpose and destiny) through faith which is at the centre of worship!

Worship Is a Way of Connecting and Responding to God

'Worship is at the centre of effective communication with God which can only be made possible by God. Worship is spiritual communication from one spirit to another Spirit. This is a realm that you can enter only if you know how to submit all that you are to your maker.'

In this realm, you are in a state of deep and selfless surrender to God. Your heart is opened to Him as you recognise the fullness of the God-head and the revelation of the finished work of Jesus.

The Holy Spirit facilitates this by empowering and transforming you. He takes you to a place where you are able to see God's beauty and humbly adore God's holiness.

In this place, your spirit man is quickened, and your will is aligned with God's will.

Your mind is nurtured with His truth. Your imagination is purified by His beauty. Your heart is filled with His joy, and you are purged of self in the beauty of His holiness. Oh, what a place to be!

Humility and Worship

Your worship should bring you to your knees in humility and total surrender as a result of your acknowledgement of the superiority of God's authority!

Ezekiel described an encounter with the presence of the Lord.

> 'And behold, the glory and brilliance of the God of Israel was coming from the way of the east; and His voice was like the sound of many waters, and the earth shone with His glory.'
>
> Ezekiel 43:2

Oh, what a beauty!

If we can all experience this daily!

This is my sincere prayer for myself and all my readers that as we get a revelation and deep understanding of what this means we will all worship in expectation of this result.

'One encounter is all we need for a transformation!'

In Mathew 8: 1-2 the Bible records that Jesus came down from the mountain with a multitude of followers, but only the story of the un-known and unclean leper was established in that situation because this leper came boldly before the throne of grace and knelt down in worship. His request was granted as he met with the one who is willing to heal, deliver and transform lives.

'You may not literally see God's glory, but a true encounter must be followed by a manifestation of His glory.'

Your life must shine in reflection of His glory, there must be symbolic, substantial and significant changes

True worship yields an encounter and encounters yield a manifestation of His glory!

This was the result experienced by Cornelius in Acts 10.

Here we are introduced to Cornelius and his family a devout and God-fearing people who lived a worship lifestyle of charitable giving and prayer. The Bible records that one day he got his encounter. In this encounter received specific instruction for the void in his life. This instruction was tailored specifically for Cornelius and his household and was mirrored to his beneficiary Peter who was miles away. Peter had no choice but to follow the instruction as he also received it during his own quiet time with the Lord.

This was a distinctive encounter that changed Cornelius' destiny and that of his household forever!

The story of Hannah (1 Samuel 1) which is the story of hope, life and truth are one that we can all identify with in different aspects of our lives. If you have earnestly and urgently desired something and that very thing has been kept away from your reach, then you would be able to empathise with Hannah. If you have ever been desperate and helpless at the same time, or have been in a situation where you are being denied what you deserve, and God has allowed it to be so to your despair and the joy of your mockers; then you will understand that you need not get angry with God but get on your knees and remind Him to make all things work for your good. This is the time to be sincere with your worship.

Hannah worshipped yearly and faithfully, but God shut up her womb until the day her worship was true, so true to the point that she did not care who was watching and judging, she had one audience; God alone.

Her restlessness was misunderstood, but she worshipped, her worship was misinterpreted even by the high priest for drunkenness, but her encounter with the King of Kings was secured.

Her transformation was registered that very day, and she got her destiny and purpose fulfilled even in the place of worship.

Omnipotent God

Albeit God is omnipresent, during worship God reveals himself to you and makes you acquainted with His will and purpose concerning your life. God is able to expose the secrets of your heart or the hearts of those around you or involved with you and the situation that stands as a challenge before you.

> 'The secrets of his heart are laid bare. And so, falling on his face, he will worship God, declaring that God is really among you.'
> *1Corinthians 14:25*

In 2 Kings 18 and 19, When Sennacherib threatened Judah and defiled God by putting everyone in a state of panic and ridiculing their faith in God's ability to deliver them from the Assyrian army, king Hezekiah responded to this situation with an act of humility before God.

King Hezekiah instructed the people not to respond to their mocker because he had a better plan which involved the omnipotent ruler of all nations.

His plan was not one of great intelligence or display of human ability and power. His plan was a spiritual strategic plan which would touch the heart of the omnipotent ruler of all nations and cause victory to be released to King Hezekiah. His plan was an act of worship in which he abased himself by tearing his expensive royal robes and stripping himself of all human dignity. Hezekiah responded by stripping himself naked before God, putting on sackcloth in exchange for his wealth went to the temple which was the designated place of worship.

As a result, the Lord revealed the secret of the victory of Israel to his prophet Isaiah who was not even with Hezekiah at that time.

Do you feel under threat? The fact is if you feel under threat, the pressure is real irrespective of the category of threat you are up against.

We live in a society and in times when nothing is secure. Financial giants are failing and falling, and this is creating a ripple effect on people's health (both physical and mental), relationships and families are being strained and destroyed. People live in fear of terrorist attacks, racism and hate crime, young people are afraid of going out as there is the imminent threat of knife and gun crime, and the list goes on....

The good news is there is a worked out example for us to follow.

'We can depend on God for victory in worship!'

Hezekiah's prayer began with worship. Hezekiah prayed before the LORD and said,

> *'O LORD, the God of Israel, who is enthroned above the cherubim [of the ark in the temple], You are the God, You alone, of all the kingdoms of the earth. You have made the heavens and the earth.'*
>
> *2 Kings 19:15*

Hezekiah obtained his victory from the one who is enthroned above the cherubim, from the sovereign God who has no competition or competitor. Be of good cheer, Elohim is still enthroned!

God Is in Attendance in the Place of Worship

When in worship God is crowned again as King and you are able to see the magnitude of His Majesty in comparison to the miniaturisation your world and whatever is going on in it.

God is enthroned in our praises.

> 'But You are holy, O You who are enthroned in [the holy place where] the praises of Israel [are offered].'
>
> *Psalm 22:3*

Your praise must enthrone Him alone. Your praise must come from a holy place. Offer holy praise, from a holy place to a holy God.

The Hebrew word used here is Tehillah which is synonymous with quiet praise songs or hymns. When God is present, there must surely be a manifestation of his glory, do not be fooled, if there is no manifestation, then there is no presence.

> 'The manifestation of God's glory is beyond being slain in the spirit, falling down or any outward physical demonstration of God's presence. It is one that guarantees a transformation in the lives of those that have an encounter.'

The Bible informs us that in His presence there is fullness of joy and at His right hand are pleasures forevermore Psalm 16:11).

So one of the manifestations we should get from worship is fullness of joy, and this could be given to us in the form of the revelation of how to attain freedom from addictions and bondage; peace from our battles, joy in the midst of sorrowful seasons, rest in the midst of situations that have stirred up worry, faith when in doubt, calm and the ability to trust Him in the midst of our fears and stormy weather, the strength and ability to love when you should be bitter, and the grace to forgive even when your anger is justified.

In his presence, there should be an ignition of hope, a renewal of the mind, a shining light beckoning at the end of that horrible dark tunnel.

'We can be empowered to let go of bitterness and receive a new identity!'

We have an assurance that when we seek Him in worship, He will be found.

'But from there you will seek the LORD your God,
and you will find Him if you search for Him
with all your heart and all your soul.'
Deuteronomy 4:29

This is an assurance we have been given. Remember the Lord magnifies and exalts above all things His name and His word. His decrees surpass His fame, His promises are backed by all the honour of His name and His word is consistent with His name (Psalm 138:2).

The Presence of God and Change

When God is present, there must be change because he is the ancient of days that never changes but changes all situations, when God is present there must be healing and deliverance that is why the great commission commands all believers to be involved in the healing and deliverance ministry.

'And He said to them, 'Go into all the world and preach the
gospel to all creation.

16 He who has believed [in Me] and has been baptized will be
saved [from the penalty of God's wrath and judgment]; but he
who has not believed will be condemned.

17 These signs will accompany those who have believed: in My
name they will cast out demons, they will speak in new tongues;

18 they will pick up serpents, and if they drink anything deadly, it will not hurt them; they will lay hands on the sick, and they will get well.'

Mark 16:15-18

'Healing occurs both physically and psychologically in God's presence.'

You might receive the grace to forgive that person that has caused you to live a bitter life. You may receive insight to a particular truth that will open an amazing chapter in your journey, you might receive conviction to stop a particular habit that is making you ill, you might receive a deep revelation about a project or even the faith to believe that you can do it or be healed.

Your manifestation may result in deliverance from a broken heart and affliction, you might find refuge and rest in God, it could be a revelation on how to serve the Lord with gladness and learn not to focus on your troubles and the ability to forsake your wicked ways.

There is always something tangible for everyone who gets an encounter, seeks for an encounter during worship and your expectation will result in joy.

The Presence and the Power of God

'The presence of God is the power of God.'

If God is present, rest assured you have the ability to be delivered from all limitations and embargoes on your life be them God ordained, self-inflicted or man-made.

We must be aware that affliction can be God ordained due to his anger incurred by sin or due to Him abandoning you.

'For a brief moment I abandoned you, But with great compassion and mercy I will gather you [to Myself again].'

Isaiah 54:7

In the book of Jonah chapter 1, Jonah's disobedience resulted in affliction and this affliction from the Lord affected everyone around him. The crew discovered they had done nothing to deserve this affliction and they recognised it was from the Lord. They only received their deliverance after worshipping God.

Similarly, Jonah received his deliverance from the belly of the whale after he worshipped. His prayer was worship focused. This caused the Lord to move, the Lord gave a specific instruction to the whale and the whale vomited Jonah in the right location and position to enable Jonah to complete his assignment. Jonah was not sick or lost. Worship is the key!

Deliverance which when simply put is the ability to be set free from bondage or whatever is holding you back or to be liberated from your limitations cannot take place without the power of God.

'God is a merciful God who is willing to gather us back again.'

So be of good cheer if He has forgiven you and set you free then you are free indeed.

'Stop caging yourself; adapt to your new given freedom!'

'The greatest form of slavery is in the mind because even after emancipation the individual is unable to adapt to freedom.'

Try and picture the scenario of a lion and its trainer. The most disheartening truth is that the caged/ tamed lion ends up doing tricks taught to it by its trainer, and is unaware of the depth of its strength.

Here we see the lion who is the so-called king of the jungle subject itself to a physically weaker species whose strength is derived from manipulation.

Because the trainer has mastered the art of manipulating the lion to believe the trainer is stronger, the lion will never be free to explore or experience its natural potential but will trade it with the imposed potential which is the agenda of the trainer.

The tragedy is this lion may not be able to adapt to the wild ever again depending on the amount of psychological disempowerment if has faced when it is released.

Animals that have been caged for a long time in a zoo or any regulated environment find it extremely hard to adapt to the wild when rescued and released. If released at the end of its lifespan it might be more harmful to it than good.

But thanks be to God that we are not animals but sons and joint heirs of the kingdom!

Thanks be to God that there is room for the prodigal son in his father's house!

Thanks be to God that there is also the reconciliation party on the first day of his return

Thanks be to God that there is also a reinstating celebration to show everyone present (even the self-righteous, judgemental and bitter brother) that the wrongdoer has been restored fully to the family where he will be provided with all he needs for inclusion and the rest of the journey ahead.

God is the only one that can offer divine assistance from the damage caused by destiny and purpose manipulators. Just like the tamed lion, without God's intervention after you have been released from the hands of the evil manipulators, you will not be able to understand your assignment, recognise your purpose of fulfilling your destiny.

All glory to the Father of all lights who is able to intervene and shine His light in all dark areas and also make people whole!

'God is in the business of restoration which can be attained in worship!'

The presence of God is the power of God and Moses understood this that is why he refused other forms of divine assistance.

'And Moses said to Him, 'If Your presence does not go [with me], do not lead us up from here.'

Exodus 33:15

'Worship attracts the intimate and complete divine assistance which can only occur when God is present!'

God Speaks in Worship

When God is present, he speaks and does the impossible.

'The voice of the LORD is powerful;
The voice of the LORD is full of majesty.
The voice of the LORD breaks the cedars;
Yes, the LORD breaks in pieces the cedars of Lebanon.

He makes Lebanon skip like a calf,
And Sirion (Mount Hermon) like a young, wild ox.

The voice of the LORD rakes flames of fire (lightning).

The voice of the LORD shakes the wilderness;
The LORD shakes the wilderness of Kadesh.

The voice of the LORD makes the doe labour and give birth
And strips the forests bare;
And in His temple, all are saying, 'Glory!'

Psalm 29:4-9

When Simon had an encounter with Jesus' presence, Jesus spoke to Simon and changed his name from Simon which means 'God has heard' to Peter which means 'stone or rock' to signify the role that Peter will play in the church.

When Saul had his encounter, he (Saul) renounced his Hebrew name which means 'asked for or prayed for' and picked up his Latin name Paul which means 'little/small or humble' as a result of the transformation and his assignment he was about to embark upon to the Gentiles.

Both of them had different encounters and received divine direction for their assignment, purpose and destiny.

> 'As you worship, ask God for the ability to hear His voice clearly so you will be able to understand your mandate which is your personal assignment and purpose and fulfil your role in destiny.'

Peter's assignment was to be the rock on which the church would be built, and Paul was the apostle sent to the Gentiles.

Two different people
Two different encounters
Two different apostles emerged
Two different assignments
Two different mandates
Two different purposes
Two different destinies
One voice of the Lord!

True Worship Overtakes You

When you are deep in worship, it should take you to a place where, there is such awe that goes beyond human comprehension, here, man ceases and God takes over!

> 'so that the priests could not remain standing to minister because of the cloud; for the glory and brilliance of the LORD filled the house of God.'
>
> *2Chronicles 5:14*

When deep in worship, you would know that it is time to surrender and align your will with God.

There are so many people who have left lucrative professions in surrender to God's call without regret.

If you are unsatisfied with your life, surrender all to God in worship and align your will with His.

He is Alpha and Omega and is able to lead you correctly

'Worship provokes a shaking of doorposts and thresholds!'

*'At the sound of their voices, the doorposts and thresholds shook
and the temple was filled with smoke!'
(New International Version)*

Isaiah 6:4

All the doors and thresholds that have held you in will be shaken as you worship the Lord, you are his temple, and the smoke of your sacrifice will rise up to Him in Jesus' mighty name.

Worship Provokes the Shaking of the Foundations of Prisons

Worship causes doors to open by force via a violent earthquake!

Worship can break chains, in the very presence of oppressors and enemies so much so that they have no option but to recognise the power of the God and submit to Him.

*'But about midnight when Paul and Silas were praying and
singing hymns of praise to God, and the prisoners were listening
to them;*

*26 suddenly there was a great earthquake, so [powerful] that the
very foundations of the prison were shaken and at once all the
doors were opened and everyone's chains were unfastened.*

*27 When the jailer, shaken out of sleep, saw the prison doors
open, he drew his sword and was about to kill himself, thinking
that the prisoners had escaped.*

²⁸ But Paul shouted, saying, 'Do not hurt yourself, we are all here!'

²⁹ Then the jailer called for torches and rushed in, and trembling with fear he fell down before Paul and Silas.'

Acts 16:25-29

'Midnight is a time of dramatic change, there is a transition and an end to one era in time and a beginning of another simultaneously.'

'Midnight is a very significant time for God to respond to your worship!'

'Captivity is a good place to worship as people tend to focus when in captivity.'

One is able to be void of all the daily distractions that mask truths represented by the hustle and bustle of life.

In captivity, reality sets in, and you have no escape route.

There are a wide variety of coping mechanisms in captivity some negative techniques include denial, self-pity, anger, revenge, violence which would only trigger an equally negative response from your captors as they will invent better ways of holding you down and making you submit to their will.

Some positive approaches to coping in captivity include:

Recognition of the fact that you are in bondage,

Reflection on the journey and discovering the choices and the practices or carelessness that led you to bondage,

Having a strategic plan for escape; sometimes you need a long term and a short term plan to escape and would need to set realistic milestones in proportion to your faith and actions.

You also need hope and motivation as they are vital ingredients for change.

When in captivity with a positive attitude, your positive attitude will intrigue your captors, make them think you are not a threat and take them off guard.

Just because you are born again and spirit filled does not shield you from captivity if that is the case then Paul and Silas should not have been held captive neither should Peter and other great apostles.

Paul and Silas were able to get their release from captivity via worship. Even their captors turned to God! What a magnificent testimony!

Sometimes rather than complain, moan, bind, loose, rebuke, resist, scream, get bitter, rebel, hate God, hate everyone, be isolated and entertain all those negative and useless states of affairs you can think of, just worship God and see the manifestation of his promises!

His promises are yes and amen (2 Corinthians 1:20), and he instructs us to rejoice always and again (Philippians 4:4).

The psalmist David got this revelation and decided to be in a state of rejoicing, he decided he would choose to bless the Lord at all times! (Psalm 34:1)

Worship Convicts

In the same story of imprisonment and divine liberation featured in the book of Acts chapter 16, there were some bystanders who were listening to Paul and Silas worshipping in spirit and in truth.

God was present, and there was a manifestation of the power of God which resulted in Paul and Silas' deliverance from captivity, restoration to freedom that will enable them to carry out their assignment, achieve the purpose and fulfil destiny.

It also led to salvation and a conviction for the jailer and all the by-standers watching the worshippers!

This one experience changed so many lives forever!

> "Your worship should intrigue bystanders in your life and bring them to God.'

Worship delivered a whole nation from their strong enemy!

Worship sends out missiles to the camp of the enemy,

Confusion is a weapon of mass destruction used by God to defeat the enemies of His people.

Sometimes you do not have to fight back!

Your worship is deadlier than you understand.

Your worship has a wide variety of strategies that are released against strong enemies.

> 'When he had consulted with the people, he appointed those who sang to the LORD and those who praised Him in their holy (priestly) attire, as they went out before the army and said, 'Praise and give thanks to the LORD, for His mercy and loving kindness endure forever.'
>
> 22 When they began singing and praising, the LORD set ambushes against the sons of Ammon, Moab, and Mount Seir, who had come against Judah; so they were struck down [in defeat].
>
> 23 For the sons of Ammon and Moab [suspecting betrayal] rose up against the inhabitants of Mount Seir, completely destroying them; and when they had finished with the inhabitants of Seir, they helped to destroy one another.'
>
> *2 Chronicles 20:21-23*

Who is your strong enemy?

Sometimes it could be you. Worship will help you put things into perspective and put God on the throne.

You can be delivered from pride, foolishness, unbelief, ignorance, laziness, lack of vision and drive, de-motivation, short sited vision, impatience, poor character, negative personality, greed, immorality and other strongholds if you see yourself as nothing and God as everything.

Worship Puts Your Enemies to Shame

The prophets of Baal in 1kings 18:16-40 were put to shame and no amount of shouting and self-mutilation yielded any results.

The Prophet Elijah's prayer was infused with worship and the Lord proved Himself to be the only God!

> 'At the time of the offering of the evening sacrifice, Elijah the prophet approached [the altar] and said, 'O LORD, the God of Abraham, Isaac, and Israel (Jacob), let it be known today that You are God in Israel and that I am Your servant and that I have done all these things at Your word.
> 37 Answer me, O LORD, answer me, so that this people may know that You, O LORD, are God, and that You have turned their hearts back [to You].'
>
> *1Kings 18:36-37*

Add worship to your prayer requests.

Elijah acknowledged God, Elijah approached the altar rendering adulation and honour to the God of Abraham, Isaac and Israel.

Our Lord Jesus replicated this pattern when he taught us how to pray in Mathew 6:9

> 'Pray, then, in this way: 'Our Father who is in heaven, Hallowed be Your name.'

The name of the Lord must be hallowed in all you do!

If you need your enemies to be made an open show of by Jehovah Sabaoth then worship Him more.

The message in our Lord's Prayer is simple:

Worship the Lord God only
Worship before you ask for your daily bread
Worship before you ask for forgiveness
Worship before you ask for protection
Worship before you ask for deliverance.

'God will always arise when the enemy defiles His name.
He is the only one who fights His own battle.'

We can see this also in the story of David and Goliath. Goliath said:

'I defy the battle lines of Israel this day, give me a man so we may fight together.'
1Samuel 17:10, 45

David told Goliath that he had come in the name of the God of the armies of Israel whom Goliath had mocked and God arose and defended His name thereby putting the whole attacking nation of Philistine to shame.

'The battle is the Lords, you cannot fight it on your own, but you can fight it on your knees in worship!'

Worship Causes Gates to Be Lifted up and Everlasting Doors to Be Open so that the King of Glory Can Come and Reign!

Many times during life's journey, we find ourselves in a tight corner because of the short-sighted choices we made, Either due to impatience, ignorance, foolishness, pressure, the environment or circle we were in at the time, lack of resources, no knowledge of God and His plan for us, not seeking God's will but satisfying our lusts and much more.

What life choices/patterns have kept you locked in the prison of life?

What life patterns have kept you limited and blinded?

'Your transformation is in the power of worship!'

The Psalmist got to a place in life that he had to reassure himself through worship that God was and is still in control. He reaffirmed his faith and his victory, he reminded himself of the criteria to go into the presence of the Lord in worship.

He laid a claim on his right to be blessed, not just him but his posterity.

Then he declared to his limitations to shift so that God can be glorified.

He understood that God could not share the same habitation with his long-term limitations, habits, beliefs, choices and all those things that had exalted themselves as king over his life. He declared and worshipped:

> 'Lift up your heads, O gates, And be lifted up, ancient doors,
> That the King of glory may come in.
>
> 8 Who is the King of glory? The LORD strong and mighty, The
> LORD mighty in battle.
>
> 9 Lift up your heads, O gates, And lift them up, ancient doors,
> That the King of glory may come in.
>
> 10 Who is [He then] this King of glory? The LORD of hosts, He is
> the King of glory [who rules over all creation with His heavenly
> armies]. Selah'
>
> *Psalm 24:7-9*

'rayer Infused with Worship Can Raise the Dead

Our Lord Jesus Christ at the tomb of Lazarus demonstrated this. Remember that Lazarus had been dead for a while and decomposition had set in.

Before burial, there are always certain rituals that people do irrespective of your background and culture. We don't just dump dead bodies in the bin or on the streets.

Firstly you must be convinced that death has occurred.

Preferably medically, I would like to imagine that in communities where there are no medical facilities, there are certified ways of confirming that death has occurred.

Only after this, do you prepare the body for burial, and finally lay it to rest.

Do you realise that we can do this with our dreams and aspirations in life? Sometimes we even do this with our assignment, purpose and destiny. Just because we are unable to see how they can come to realisation or just because the procedure and processes whereby they can be achieved are full of mountains, valleys, deserts, oceans, rocks, storms and all manners of obstacles; we decide to certify our dreams and aspirations dead. We proceed to prepare them for burial, we convincingly lay them to rest and finally roll a huge stone over them!

Some of us have buried some of your dreams and aspirations because we tried once and failed.

Some of us are so overwhelmed with pain and confusion that we have decided to lay our assignments, purposes and destinies to rest and have decided to settle for less. We have compromised the dreams we had traded in the visions that we wrote down and are okay to just get by daily.

We have buried them for so long that they have started to decompose!

The thing about a decomposed body is that it oozes and provides a stench to anyone who comes anywhere close to where it is. The stench makes people uncomfortable, and they begin to search for it and have no peace till it is found, uncovered, exposed and put in its appropriate place.

If you have buried your dream, vision, assignment, purpose or destiny, it will affect you in such a way that you would be so restless until you begin to take steps towards finding your place.

Your spirit man will be troubled and restless; people around you will mention your abilities and qualities to you that match with your deep desires. This is the time to search, find, uncover, expose and fit into your place. I speak from experience.

'If you are feeling unfulfilled, you must engage in soul searching!'

This is not for everyone. Decomposed bodies in the graveyard do not have the same effect as those buried in shallow graves or those hidden. The decomposed bodies in the graveyard do not stink the place out.

I have gone to a few funerals, and the graveyard does not stink.

So if you are in your place, you will not be restless!

To God be the glory that we have the example of our Lord Jesus Christ.

By the tomb of Lazarus, Jesus made it clear to us that all things are possible to those who believe. Jesus was motivated by the love he had for Lazarus' family. You should be motivated by the love you had for those dreams when you first conceived them.

Jesus had a reason not to go back to Judea as the Jews were plotting to stone him, but this did not stop him from going to resurrect Lazarus.

What is stopping you from resurrecting your dreams?

Martha misunderstood Jesus' mission, but Jesus did not give up or forsake the mission.

During the process of resurrecting your dreams and hopes, you will be misunderstood and misjudged but don't let this stop you.

When Jesus saw the effect of death, he was deeply moved in his spirit to the point of anger by the sorrow caused by death. Today Jesus is still deeply moved by the sorrow caused by the death of your dreams, your hopes, your purpose and your assignment. This revelation should motivate you to be moved to a point when you can take action.

Just as Jesus asked for the location of the dead body, you too must locate that dream.

Just as Jesus wept, weeping over your buried dream is okay, but it is not enough. It is okay to express your emotions, however, what do you do after you have wept over your excuses?

Jesus was even advised by Martha, the dead man's sister not to bother with the resurrection plan due to the stench and offence that this will cause to the community.

Are you afraid of the effect of revisiting your dream on your circle of influence?

Are you behind held back by what you think people will say or think about you?

It is time to take action! You will never know the results or the impact you can make. You will never know for certain what heights you can attain unless you do something about that situation.

Some people laughed at Jesus and mocked him even at the entrance of the tomb, but he went on right ahead, He worshipped our Father, He gave thanks and took action; He instructed them to roll the stone away and completed His assignment, purpose and destiny regarding Lazarus.

> *'And Jesus raised His eyes [toward heaven] and said, 'Father, I thank You that You have heard Me.*
>
> *42 I knew that You always hear Me and listen to Me; but I have said this because of the people standing around, so that they may believe that You have sent Me [and that You have made Me Your representative].'*
>
> *43 When He had said this, He shouted with a loud voice, ' Lazarus, come out!'*
>
> *John 11:41-43*

Jesus glorified His Father that is worship. Infuse your prayer with worship, believe again, hope again, have faith again, reassure yourself of God's love and ability to answer your prayers. Find out what you need to know again, empower yourself again, take action again, revisit the tomb of your dream, assignment, purpose and destiny in worship and God in his faithfulness will make way for you. Speak life to your dreams, and they will resurrect!

> *'You will never know how far you can go unless you start walking.'*

Rise up, begin to take those baby steps, give yourself a chance!

A Mighty Warrior

Worship makes you understand that God is a mighty warrior.

In the book of Exodus, the Lord fought a mighty battle for the children of Israel and won with awesome signs and wonders to the glory of His name and the shame of Pharaoh.

The final battle ended in the red sea.

The final battle silenced Pharaoh forever and there was no more mention of this great enemy and his reign after the final battle!

When God fights for you, he makes it the final battle and when you come out in victory, you will need no one to explain that you have a mighty warrior for a father.

When God gives you rest from all your troubles, you will know that you have overcome the final hurdle and it has been by the hand of the Lord so you cannot boast about your part in it.

You will have no choice but to proclaim Him for all to see.

Moses who was their leader, who has spent time with God and understands how to reach the heart of the father decided to respond to this awesome victory in worship.

In chapter 15 we see Moses compose a song of victory and worship after experiencing the strategic defeat put together by the mighty warrior and ruler of the hosts of heaven in action!

This was a revelation of another side of God; he had never experienced God like this before even though he had spent a lot of time with the King of Kings receiving specific instructions for deliverance.

He had never experienced the Almighty warrior execute total victory, and he responds thus, in verse 3

'The LORD is a warrior; The LORD is His name!'

In Joshua 5:13-14, the angel that encountered Joshua informed Joshua that he (the angel) was there as a captain of the army of the Lord. He was there on military business with an order from The Commander In Chief!

My father was a Colonel in the Nigerian Army and we lived in the military barracks till I was 18/19, so I have an understanding of how the army affects those affiliated with it. They had a slogan 'obey the last order.' My father was just one individual in the army but if he went anywhere on official business his presence represented the whole of the Nigerian Army put together. He was saluted, respected and obeyed and in return, he served with all diligence and followed all orders from the Commander In Chief who was the Head of States as well!

God is the Commander in Chief Of The Hosts Of Heaven.

You must have a level of experience, tenacity and other qualities to rise up to certain ranks in the army. God is omnipotent and is the mighty warrior who is great in every battle.

Your worship will provoke help from this warrior!

You will receive news of pending victory and an assurance of godly assistance when you worship. In 2 Chronicles 20 Jehoshaphat received news about the great imminent attack upon his nation and full of fear, he decided to worship.

He exalted the name of the Lord in his prayer; his prayer was an awesome worship, he asked God questions and reassured himself of Gods power and ability to deliver his nation from the situation. In verse 6 he prayed and worshipped.

> 'O LORD, God of our fathers, are You not God in heaven? And do You not rule over all the kingdoms of the nations? Power and might are in Your hand, there is no one able to take a stand against You.

Immediately after the prayer, he received an answer from the Lord. In verses 14-15

> 'the Spirit of the LORD came upon Jahaziel .... 15 He said, 'Listen carefully, all [you people of] Judah, and you inhabitants of Jerusalem, and King Jehoshaphat. The LORD says this to you: 'Be not afraid or dismayed at this great multitude, for the battle is not yours, but God's.

Jahaziel provided divine instructions and direction for victory from the Lord. In verse 15 the Lord told the people clearly that the battle was His and not theirs. After receiving this comforting assurance, they worshipped again. The next day they carried on in worship, and the Lord went ahead to display his military ability, he strategized against the enemies of His people and set ambushes against them.

He caused these enemies to receive an instruction that mobilised them against each other.

The strategy used by God totally destroyed and annihilated the enemies of his beloved children, and they worshipped after the battle.

I do not know what enemy you are facing, I do not know what evil partnership has been formed against you, by you, or for your sake or which Pharaoh is boasting regarding you saying like they said to Moses:

'I will pursue, I will overtake, I will divide the spoil; My desire shall be satisfied against them; I will draw my sword, my hand shall dispossess them and drive them out.'

Exodus 15:19

All I know is that your worship can provoke and invoke divine help!!

Your worship can cause the Commander in Chief Of The Hosts Of Heaven to strategize!

Your worship can cause God to issue an order of confusion into the camp of the enemy!

I can assure you that as you worship, your enemies will definitely be put to shame and you will have a reason to compose a song of victory!

You do not need to wait until you receive the news of imminent attack or danger before you begin worshipping, however, if you have received this news and are fearful, be encouraged; Jehoshaphat was fearful, but that did not stop him from worshipping.

Dear friend when faced with a battle, encourage yourself in the Lord as David did at the battle of Ziklag.

'Even after you have suffered loss encourage yourself in the Lord!'

'Perspective is everything!'

'Remain focused; God has not finished with you yet!'

David was greatly distressed due to the reality of the total loss that seemed to confront him on his return.

His family and all those he left behind had been taken away to be enslaved, this was the plan of the enemy, but God was not in agreement.

Sometimes we are at a standstill at the road block of the enemy.

The reality when we arrive at this terrible place is so negative and degrading that it is only human to lose focus on the mighty warrior.

The evidence presented before us is so severe, gigantic and overwhelmingly painful and real to us at that moment in time because we have seen or experienced the plan and power of the enemy, however, the good news is that God is not in agreement as this is not God's plan!

If David did not pursue God's plan after experiencing the enemy's plan, he would have missed it and lost all.

Everyone around David was embittered, and there was talk of stoning their greatly loved and respected leader as a result of the disappointment and the loss they had suffered through his leadership.

Their homes had been burned down, their families are taken away to be enslaved; they had lost everything of value.

Have you lost everything as a result of dwelling under a particular leader? Have you lost everything regarding that career that you invested so much time and effort in just to be made redundant with minimal benefits?

Have you invested so much in that relationship and it has now ended in hurt and shame?

Has all your money, time and effort gone as a result of your business partner's leadership?

Have you lost your home, children, self-esteem and confidence as a result of your husband's or wife's actions?

Or maybe it is you who have lead people into the plan of the enemy.

If God the mighty warrior is aware of that situation you need not lament any further, He is waiting to give you divine instruction.

David turned a deaf ear to all the vengeful and hurtful reports coming from his followers, and after crying till he could cry no more, he encouraged himself in the Lord and sought the face of God.

My dear friend after it seems as if the plan of the enemy has been accomplished concerning you, wipe your tears and ask God for his blueprint!

'There is always victory when the mighty warrior fights for you.'

Worship before the battle!
Worship in the battle!
Worship after the battle because God is faithful and remains faithful at all times!

Worship Brings Deliverance from Sin, Salvation and Peace

In Luke chapter 7 there is a story of a woman who was famous for the wrong reasons. She was so famous that she was recognised for her actions and was described so.

Is it not interesting how people chose to label her 'sinner' and 'notorious?'

Irrespective of their labels, she was able to receive a blessing from our Lord Jesus Christ.

Her worship made her the only one with the right attitude in that gathering and led her to receive her deliverance from that sin which had drawn attention to her and given her a label.

She received her deliverance from her sin in the presence of her haters and mockers!

While they were busy assessing her and passing judgement, her worship was approved, and she was set free!

Just because her sin was obvious to all, they chose to focus on labelling her and discriminating against her to make themselves feel good.

They used her standard as a licence to remain in theirs!

I am sure the place was filled with a wide variety of secret sins.

If we had a screen that displayed the state of our affairs to us for all to see (like the Telly-Tubbies I am assuming we are all conversant with those children television characters), most people would never leave the house!

However, this awesome woman who had her whole life on display on a screen for all to see; did not let that hinder her. Instead, she set aside her foolish pride and worshipped at Jesus' feet. Verse 37 tells the story:

> *37 'Now there was a woman in the city who was [known as] a sinner; and when she found out that He was reclining at the table in the Pharisee's house, she brought an alabaster vial of perfume; 38 and standing behind Him at His feet, weeping, she began wetting His feet with her tears, and wiped them with the hair of her head, and [respectfully] kissed His feet [as an act signifying both affection and submission] and anointed them with the perfume.'*

She did a prophetic act of worship and submission that yielded deliverance and salvation while her critics remained the same!

Her story of deliverance was the only one recorded in that gathering, even the host (Simon) missed his opportunity to receive, and he ended up exchanging his visitation for a platform for the woman's glory!

The divine visitation which was loaded with the power of transformation that came specifically to him was of no effect to him.

The once in a lifetime opportunity meant to change him did not change him as he was busy being a critic and a judge.

When worship was needed, his was nowhere to be found.

So instead of the visitation to result in a positive transformation for him, the visitation transformed the worshipper and God's promise for transformation did not return to God void!

The designated and dispatched transformation needed worship for it to become a reality and only the worship of the 'sinner' and 'notorious' woman was available.

Her worship changed her life and restored peace to her.

Jesus told her in verses 48 and 50:

> *'Your sins are forgiven.' ......'Your faith [in Me] has saved you; go in peace [free from the distress experienced because of sin].'*

Worship Changes Lives

In Luke 8 we see the story of the woman with the issue of blood; we see how her bowing down in worship met with a reaction of healing power from Jesus that transformed her life.

This woman bowed down in faith and worship to reach the hem of His garment knowing that He was God and He rewards those who diligently seek him.

I am sure she had been seeking otherwise she would not have known where Jesus was!

The Bible tells us how she came up trembling, fell down before Jesus and declared in the presence of all the people the reason why she had touched the hem of His garment, she also gave her testimony of immediately healing right in front of her audience.

This is the same audience who was wondering why Jesus was insistent that power to heal had gone out of Him, the same audience that questioned the integrity of Jesus the King. In verse 48:

'He said to her, 'Daughter, your faith [your personal trust and confidence in Me] has made you well. Go in peace (untroubled, undisturbed well-being).'

'Your worship can cause power to leave the throne and come to you.'

Are you seeking for God's supernatural intervention? Be a worshipper!

Worship Puts Your Hand on the Necks of Your Enemies

'Judah, you are the one whom your brothers shall praise; Your hand will be on the neck of your enemies; Your father's sons shall bow down to you.'
Gen 49:8

Judah was preferred amongst his brothers because his mother Leah had sown praise to Jehovah Elohim when she gave birth to him. She did this by naming him praise! She did not let her past or present troubles deter her. She sowed a memorial seed that can never be eradicated by calling her son Praise. She personified her praise, and this remains till date.

This seed made him receive a special blessing from his dying father and subsequently enabled him to overtake his brothers and placed him at an unprecedented advantage over them.

His assignment, purpose and destiny were birthed out of the sacrificial praise rendered to God by Leah at his birth.

Judah developed into a mighty and significant tribe which played awesome roles throughout destiny. They got the best land, produced the first Judge and numerous kings, including King David; they even produced the ultimate King out Lord Jesus Christ!

David and Solomon's hands were always on the neck of their enemies.

History depicts our Lord Jesus Christ was a product of that lineage.

The fourth child whose birth brought forth praise from his mother turned out to produce the Messiah and today at the mention of the name of Jesus, every knee must bow.

Worship Rendered in a Simple and Pure Form Produces Strength that Silences the Foes and Avengers

Psalm 8:2 tells us that God ordains strength out of the mouths of babes and infants because of His enemies so that He (God) can silence both the enemy and the avenger.

Remember God's strength is showcased in our weaknesses!

Worship puts an end to violence, devastation and destruction brought to you by the enemy and the avenger of sin. Satan is the accuser of the brethren and keeps on pushing for a guilty verdict with the maximum sentence as this will provide him with the opportunity to kill, steal and destroy your mandate, assignment, purpose and destiny. Satan is forever ready to wrought violence, devastation, destruction and tragedy. He is on a mission and is not ready or willing to spare you.

Your worship will trigger mercy. The blood of Jesus is the only plea we have and need in the courtroom of the Lord which can exonerate. God is a merciful judge, and worship will give you your portion out of the multitude of God's tender mercies.

When you live a lifestyle of worship the walls of your life would be the awesome work of salvation by Jesus, these walls will shield you from danger, invasion and defilement.

These walls will make your life a safe haven because the name of the Lord is a strong tower for the righteous to find safety against the calamities and arrows hurled from the pit of hell.

Isaiah 60:18 tells us that violence will not be heard again in the land whose walls are called salvation; neither will devastation or destruction be able to penetrate the borders of a land or city whose gates are called praise.

'When you rename all your access and entry points of your destiny PRAISE, life will never be the same again.'

When you approach life in faith with the view and understanding that all things are working together for your good, since God is in control of your life due to salvation. You will be able to live the scripture that instructs you to give thanks in everything because you understand that this is the will of God in Christ Jesus concerning.

This will result in you living a lifestyle where you praise in and out of season.

You will praise when going out and when coming in.

You will praise for everything that comes in through your gates of life and for everything that goes out of your gates because you remember the promise that assures you to always receive good.

This is how you can rename your gates and your walls!

Once your gates and walls have been renamed, it will be impossible for violence to enter into your land neither will it be possible for devastation and destruction to enter your borders.

When your gates and walls are renamed, you will find rest and peace in God knowing that He is faithful and has good thoughts to bring you to the end He expects you to get to.

He is indeed able to see you through and help you to identify your assignment, work out your purpose and fulfil your destiny if you allow Him to be your compass.

> 'You cannot afford to stop praising because you have encountered setbacks.'

If you are aware of who the Bishop of your soul is then, you must keep on marching on and never lose your sound.

Missile

Worship is the missile that executes vengeance upon the enemy, punishes them, binds kings with chains and nobles with fetters of iron and gives honour to the saints of God.

> 'Let the high praises of God be in their throats,
> And a two-edged sword in their hands,
>
> 7 To execute vengeance on the nations
> And punishment on the peoples,
>
> 8 To bind their kings with chains
> And their nobles with fetters of iron,
>
> 9 To execute on them the judgment written.
> This is the honour for all His godly ones. Praise the LORD!
> (Hallelujah!)'
>
> *Psalm 149:6-9*

Whatever has been enthroned as 'king' over your situation whether now or over a long period of time will be dethroned as you worship.

Whatever you have enthroned as 'king' in God's stead will also be dethroned as you worship in perspective.

We have been given an assured honour so begin to worship and let God's words be perfected in your life, let His promises be yeah and amen concerning you and let judgment be executed over the enemy of your progress and soul.

Instruments

Worshipping with instruments causes the Lord to strike the enemy with his punishing rod and fight them with the blows of his arm.

> 'And every blow of the rod of punishment, Which the LORD will lay on them, Will be to the music of Israel's tambourines and lyres; And in battles, brandishing weapons, He will fight Assyria.'
>
> *Isaiah 30:32*

It is really important to ensure you have time for instrumental worship as well this is a sound that is pleasing to God. This is also an avenue where worship that is expressed beyond words is offered. This kind of worship is unadulterated as all it contains is the sounds made by man on instruments to ministers to God. Individuals have their favourite sounds, I love music but not all genres so I will only respond to the genre that ticks my box. This is not so with the King over every sound. Each sound has a spiritual implication and meaning; each sound produces a distinctive result.

Your Lyrics

As a songwriter and worship leader, I am particular about the lyrics I write and the lyrics of my worship song list. I am sure you will agree with me that there are some 'carnally' written lyrics that do not give

God any glory and there are some 'spiritually' written lyrics that give Him glory and remain timeless classics.

The prophet Isaiah renders a song of praise to God in chapter 25 of his book. He proclaims in worship a catalogue of reasons why our God is worthy of praise such as God's miracles, perfect faithfulness, relentless strength which causes terrible and violent nations to tremble in fear.

He goes ahead to reveal God's ability to be a stronghold to the helpless and the poor in distress, a shelter from the storm and a shade from the heat, to subdue the noise of the foreigners and silence the song of the tyrants.

He assures us that our God is able to provide us with choice delicacies on the mountain, He is able to destroy shrouds that cloud and rip apart sheets that cover nations, communities and families.

There are 'veils' embedded in different cultures that separate people from God; that destroys lives and incites hatred in communities.

Some of these 'veils' ignore corruption, poverty and promote selfishness. Some excuse away immorality and reckless living resulting in pain, suffering, distress, tragedy and disdain in numerous communities.

If people could respond to God in worship, we would have a different outcome. If the church would stop being selfish and pray for communities and nations, there could be a culture shift from what it is today.

Furthermore, he speaks of God's ability to swallow up death, wipe tears from all faces and take away disgrace!

I do not know what God has done for you in the past or what you are facing at the moment but can I submit to you that a God who can do the above and more is worthy of your praise and your worship!

As a parent, I am limited regarding what I can do for my children because I cannot be with them all the time and cannot fulfil every want, desire or need that they possess. The best I can do for them is raise them right in the way and fear of the Lord, provide them with the essential tools for life, expose them to the best opportunities, train them to identify opportunities that are presented to them and make the best of these opportunities.

As a human being, I do not have the ability to shield them from the emotional challenges entwined in different stages and seasons of life however I can train them on how to deal with, endure and overcome these challenges respectively.

Money cannot exempt us from the different seasons of life or from the many challenges that life will bring to each and every one of us. Money can only help us navigate some of our way through. For example, money cannot shield you from disease, but money can get you the best care. The irony is money cannot guarantee your response to the care or shield you from the emotional trauma deep within when facing the disease

Salvation cannot shield you from the effects of living daily in a fallen world, but it can provide the grace needed for you to go through life victoriously.

Instead of focusing on your challenges, find reasons that are real to you and if you cannot find any appreciate God for the daily miracle of waking up sane! If you were insane, you would have no reason to moan anyway!

Appreciate God for the miracles he has done in the lives of people you know or for what He has done in the bible because it gives us all the assurance that if it is recorded, then it is possible for God to do it again. You can also simply thank God for who He is.

> 'You can always find an excellent reason to see God as a God who is worthy to be praised and worshipped if you look.'

His worthiness is declared in Revelations 7:10-12:

> *'and in a loud voice they cried out, saying, 'Salvation [belongs] to our God who is seated on the throne, and to the Lamb [our*

salvation is the Trinity's to give, and to God the Trinity we owe our deliverance]. ¹¹ *And all the angels were standing around the throne and around the [twenty-four] elders and the four living creatures; and they fell to their faces before the throne and worshipped God,* ¹² *saying, 'Amen! Blessing and glory and majesty and wisdom and thanksgiving and honour and power and might belong to our God forever and ever. Amen.'*

Battle Quarters

Worship causes God to come and set up his battle quarters, it causes Him to come down and wage war in Mount Zion to give the enemy what they deserve! Isaiah 66:6 describes our worship from our temple (your inner man) as a battle cry.

'When all our temples combine in worship, they become an altar unto the Lord'

'The sound of an uproar from the city! A voice from the temple! The voice of the LORD, providing retribution to His enemies.'

Not only will a verdict of retribution be released against the enemies of the altar, your worship will induce the prophetic, and even you will be able to prophesy and be changed, meaning you will be able to understand your assignment, walk in your purpose and fulfil your destiny just as Saul did all because of your worship; this is deep!

'After that you will come to the hill of God where the garrison of the Philistines is; and when you come there to the city, you will meet a group of prophets coming down from the high place [of worship] with harp, tambourine, flute, and lyre before them, and they will be prophesying.
⁶ *Then the Spirit of the LORD will come upon you mightily, and you will prophesy with them, and you will be changed into another man.'*

1Sam 10:5-6

A Priest and a Prophet

In 2 Kings, we see the story of three kings coming together by their own wisdom to fight a battle. This wisdom was instigated by the King of Israel who invited the Kings of Judah and Edom to enjoin him in battle.

After seven good days of unfruitful marching in the wilderness of Edom, they came to the realisation that they needed a word from God!

It took one of their servants who is not even named in the record of the story to provide them with the information of where the prophet could be found.

> 'When in the battle do not underestimate the people
> God has placed around you as God is able to use anyone
> to fulfil His will.'

Many people have been derailed from destiny because of their foolish pride and judgemental attitude. Every person has a place and a role in life. Every leader needs followers and every follower needs a leader. Everyone has their assignment, purpose and destinies. Just because you do not understand their role does not make it more or less important to you or less real to them.

These kings would not have been able to locate the prophet Elisha but for their seemingly irrelevant servant. Even after they had been connected by their servant, Elisha only had respect for the King of Judah.

Elisha the great prophet of Jehovah Elohim understood that the kings who were kings in their own right needed the hand and power of Jehovah Elohim. Jehovah Elohim had to be glorified, and as a result, worship was sent to God via instruments.

In 2 Kings 3:15-16 Elisha asked for a harpist prior to the prophecy:

'But now bring me a musician.' And it came about while the musician played, that the hand (power) of the LORD came upon Elisha. 16 He said, 'Thus says the LORD.'

The musician worshipped via instruments and God who understands the translation of what the spirit of man says via moaning, groaning and unutterable words could understand their language

In worship, you need a priest and a prophet.

The priest in the Bible (the Hebrew word Kohen) refers to an individual set apart to fulfil specific functions and duties associated with worship, sacrifices, offerings, rituals, consultations, communicating the law, pronouncing blessings, and overseeing the general running of the tabernacle, temple and other specific sites of worship.

They also acted as mediators having their own identity.

We have a high priest Jesus Christ of Nazareth.

'Inasmuch then as we [believers] have a great High Priest who has [already ascended and] passed through the heavens, Jesus the Son of God, let us hold fast our confession [of faith and cling tenaciously to our absolute trust in Him as Savior].

Hebrews 4:14

On the other hand, the role of the prophet is a spokesperson for God.

In the Bible we see that the prophets are God's oracle used to reveal God's intention to individuals and nations alike, used to warn of dangers, to counsel, teach, direct, intercede, admonish and encourage God's people.

They always speak and make known the heart of God, bear the people's burdens and suffer many things. Prophets also explain mysteries and provide divine instructions and directions regarding what needs to be done in order to get specific desired results.

We see the prophets stand as watchmen over nations and destinies. They interpret dreams and explain the signs of the times, they challenge nations and expose evil, they execute judgement by declarations.

Move the people of God to worship Jehovah Elohim, they foretell the future, heal the sick, appoint and anoint kings, provide direction and guidance as well as initiate God's actions on earth.

In 1Corinthians 14:1 we are informed that the gift of prophecy is a superior gift and we are all encouraged to desire it. However, we must be aware that it is a superior gift with a superior price.

It is a superior gift for a superior sacrificial lifestyle.

You are for the people and for nations not for yourself, it is for the benefit of the world at large as God may send you anywhere he pleases, to one person or to nations. It comes with a superior cost indeed.

*'Pursue [this] love [with eagerness, make it your goal],
yet earnestly desire and cultivate the spiritual gifts [to be used
by believers for the benefit of the church], but especially that you
may prophesy [to foretell the future, to speak a new message
from God to the people].'*

1Corinthians 14:1

Is it not amazing that worship can trigger such a gift?

Like I said earlier if your worship does not provoke the manifestation of God's presence and power then it is empty!

Today if you call yourself a prophet ensure you are using heaven's blueprint as there is a great indignation from heaven against false prophets written in Ezekiel 13.

'God's word is the greatest prophet as it can never miss its objective concerning your assignment, purpose and destiny.'

'Your word is a lamp to my feet And a light to my path.'

Psalm 119:105

Chapter 4

Becoming a True Worshipper

*'Test and evaluate yourselves to see whether you are in the faith
and living your lives as [committed] believers. Examine yourselves
[not me]! Or do you not recognise this about yourselves [by an
ongoing experience] that Jesus Christ is in you — unless indeed
you fail the test and are rejected as counterfeit?'*

2 Corinthians 13:5

*'Deep calls to deep at the [thundering] sound of Your waterfalls;
All Your breakers and Your waves have rolled over me.'*

Psalm 42:7

The purpose of this section is not to endorse or condemn anyone but to reveal truths that will help us all develop. There is always a higher calling in Christ who is the river of life and not a lake. Remember according to the scripture above, it is His waterfalls, His breakers, His waves.

There is a bursting of a cloud or a waterspout that can violently flood, overthrow, carry off and wash away every old way of thinking in order to reveal God's expectation, or what is hidden deeply within the foundations of our existence. Remember we are created to be creatures of worship.

David wrote the above verses in sorrow when he was being stripped of all.

'It is time we strip ourselves of all so God can reign.'

Like the cliffs and coastlines, let His waves and His billows roll over you and create the design he has for your assignment, purpose and destiny.

Even when you feel overwhelmed by the crashing of the waves and the thunderous rolling of the billows, rest assured that if God is for you, no one can be against you. He is also merciful and will not allow you to perish in the processing room!

As a branch (He is the vine, and we are the branches) of this awesome river, you must keep on flowing.

A river is fresh water flowing from a source, across the surface of the land in channels. All rivers start at the highest point in an area, flow downstream, and gain more water from other streams, rivers and springs.

They also gain more water from added rainfall, and other water sources and provide food, energy, recreation, transportation routes, water for irrigation, and water for drinking; the benefits of rivers cannot be over emphasised in this book.

As a lecturer, I do observe my students when they are in the learning environment.

I have come to realise certain key elements of human behaviour which have been constant in all groups over the years; no one likes to know that they have fallen below the standard of expectation in any piece of work undertaken, be it summative or formative.

Human nature is very competitive, and everyone likes positive feedback. One of the models we have been trained to provide feedback is called the sandwich technique. Meaning we begin with praise, move on to the criticism then end with praise. The whole idea behind this theory is to reduce discomfort and anxiety as well as cushion the shock of the reality that the individual's work/effort is not up to expectation which could in some cases result in devastation, self-doubt, the urge to quit and trigger many more negative emotions or reactions.

However, there is the school of thought that believes this approach undermines your feedback as the listener tends to alienate your criticism and discount your positive feedback as well as doubt your integrity.

This school of thought prefers the transparent strategy.

This is a strategy that tells it as it is.

Sometimes we allow peers to provide peer assessment and feedback using their own work as a comparative analysis with room for improvement on both sides.

The Bible is the Christian's standard and marking scheme; ideologies that fall short of this standard should be correctly labelled. The more we acquaint ourselves with the truth, the better our output in situations and life in general. Ignorance is no excuse as this is the most popular book in the world!

In education, sometimes we allow our learners to self-assess using the correct marking criteria and an action plan for improvement. You will not be able to improve if you do not see the need to and you will not see the need to if you do not have the evidence that demonstrates you have fallen short!

Whatever you do feedback should allow you to make a change.

When faced with the reality of a situation or realisation that reveals the truth, as human beings there are a variety of ways to deal with it depending on if it is negative or positive.

Whatever you decide, please ensure it is one that helps you position yourself on the altar of worship as a relevant vessel unto honour.

This is a self-assessment project and an opportunity for you to either use the sandwich feedback method or the transparent strategy. Whatever you do, you must be honest with yourself remembering that this is your journey with God and no amount of masking will help move you on!

Your singing voice, status, knowledge of Bible verses, beauty, creativity, education, wealth and anything you can think of cannot be put on the scales when your worship is weighed!

This is the time for self-assessment, honest self-assessment the evidence and standard before you and I is the bible.

There are various ways of worship that the Bible advises us to stay away from. Some of these identified detrimental methods of worship are from ancient cultures, traditions, heresies and man-made doctrines.

They are empty and do not produce any results.

Due to the fact that we are all products of our environment, we may find ourselves practising some of these methods, however, the good news is this is not the end! Our God is a God that helps the helpless, and with the help of the Holy Spirit, he reveals the secret things thereby equipping us to overcome those futile habits/practices and adopt those healthy and fruitful practices that enable us to thrive in the God-ordained ways of worship which always produce results!

Below are some forms of worship identified in the Bible:

1. Self-satisfactory Worship

This category of worship has the effort of man as the focal point and has forgotten that worship is not for man.

It is important to understand that even though worship is by man, it is meant for God. Therefore, man or even angels should not get glory from it!

Always ensure you have an audience of one when you worship.

When your worship is self-satisfactory, you seek to satisfy your efforts and emotions.

Your focus is on what you can do and how well you can do it to your satisfaction. For example, if you are of the opinion that the more harshly you treat your body, the better your worship is or, the more humble you appear to be before people, the better your worship is then this is self-satisfactory.

You could even be driven by the praise you receive from your pastor or feedback from the congregation.

Some people are of the opinion that worship is 'better' with louder music, a more talented worship team, more entertaining and crowd percolating songs, etc.

I am sure you must have heard phrases (or even said them yourself) like the worship was so good today or the worship songs were rubbish today! This is all wrong, God's standard is not the same as ours, what God is looking for in worship is deeper than what the naked eyes can see or what the human mind can imagine it to be.

Worship cannot be self-imposed.

> 'These practices indeed have the appearance [that popularly passes as that] of wisdom in self-made religion and mock humility and severe treatment of the body (asceticism), but are of no value against sinful indulgence [because they do not honour God].'
>
> *Colossians 2:23*

Religious acts do not have any impact in worship as they are void of the power of God. These acts are unable to produce results, they cannot change who you are, heal you or open your eyes to the availability of God's grace.

They only draw you deeper into self-accreditation which does not please God or yield good fruit. We need to seek for power and grace in God alone.

Worship should be all about God. Self-satisfactory worship is made up of rules made by men and God is not impressed.

> 'This nation approaches [Me only] with their words And honours Me [only] with their lip service, But they remove their hearts far from Me, And their reverence for Me is a tradition that is learned by rote [without any regard for its meaning].'
>
> *Isaiah 29:13*

Your worship and the motive behind it should seek the approval of God only and not that of man. In all your doings never worship man, angels or any other entity.

In Revelations 22:9 the angel refused John's worship. He exclaimed that he was a fellow servant with John, his brethren and the prophets. We can see John's account as he states

'I, John, am the one who heard and saw these things. And when I heard and saw them, I fell down to worship before the feet of the angel who showed me these things.

⁹ But he said to me, 'Do not do that. I am a fellow servant with you and your brothers the prophets and with those who heed and remember [the truths contained in] the words of this book. Worship God.'

In Acts 10:25-26, Peter rejected Cornelius' worship!

²⁵ When Peter arrived, Cornelius met him, and fell down at his feet and worshipped him. 26 But Peter raised him up, saying, 'Stand up; I too am only a man.'

To free yourself from this error, get rid of all self-glorifying criteria such as I fasted, I prayed, I practised, etc. therefore the glory of the Lord came down when I was worshipping…

'We all need to come to a place of realisation that our human efforts cannot bring God's glory down!'

Our omnipresent Elohim is already everywhere and cannot be coerced by selfish and manipulative acts of men!

2. Charlatan Or Pretentious Worship

This worship style is for the audience of the worshipper.

Simply put, it is a show to please the attendees because it is centred on getting a response from the audience. The worship leader's goal is to percolate the crowd!

Whenever you make the assembling of the saints a social gathering rather than a spiritual gathering and focus on their response to your show, your worship becomes charlatan.

Whenever you are motivated by having a showbiz type of worship and excited or influenced by the amount of runs and ad-libs made by the singer(s) then your worship is charlatan.

If you are motivated by the response regarding the show you put up before you can describe your worship experience as awesome then again your worship is pretentious, any act of worship carried out with man at the centre of it is not to God.

It is of the flesh and not of God!

If your worship seeks human gratification or TV ratings, you are a hypocrite. In Mathew 15:7-9 Jesus spoke out against this when he addressed the Pharisees this is what he said:

> *'You hypocrites (play-actors, pretenders), rightly did Isaiah prophesy of you when he said, 8 'THIS PEOPLE HonourS ME WITH THEIR LIPS, BUT THEIR HEART IS FAR AWAY FROM ME. 9 'BUT IN VAIN DO THEY WORSHIP ME, FOR THEY TEACH AS DOCTRINES THE PRECEPTS OF MEN.'*

Charlatan worship is vain, this worship draws near to God on the outside, it honours God with lips, but the heart and motives are not aligned to what it appears to be.

This worship is vain and based on man's feedback. When you are worshipping, and your focus is on your voice range, your looks, or how cute you sound, etc., you must repent as you have missed it!

The Lord once said to me 'I am not interested in your key.'

This type of worship occurs when fellowships become social gatherings.

'Be a worshipper, not an entertainer!'

3. Ignoramus Worship

This is blind worship which is developed out of mimicked behaviour, worship acquired, or done out of routine rather than out of relationship or knowledge of who God is.

It is done in most religious gatherings. I use the word religious because religion focuses on the routine and takes pride in the observation of routine even when routine lacks understanding!

Unfortunately, this is what we do in some places of worship, but my prayer is that as you come to the realisation, you will sort this out swiftly and apply the necessary changes you need to ensure you no longer practice emptiness.

Some worship leaders copy others rather than being themselves.

It is such a shame that this is the case; I have seen some cases where worship leaders record runs on their phones and use them so they can sound exactly like the original singer.

Is God interested in this?

If you teach your pet parrot to speak can you have a meaningful conversation with it?

All you would end up achieving is having a pet than can cover some routine tricks!

A routine is good, but when worshipping from the heart, it may not be appropriate. We all know we can teach our bodies to do certain things out of routine and our minds could also go into a certain thought pattern and process out of routine. You cannot claim to lead people in worship when all you are doing is re-enacting a routine you practised off YouTube!

This type of worship does not come from a place of relationship with God but is abstract and does not please God. Relationship transcends deeper than the surface of routine or religion. Routine says close your eyes bow your head, raise your hands, jump, mimic your mentor, etc. but relationship says yield your heart to God and do what comes naturally to you. Relationship says to respond to the Holy Spirit inside of you.

It's about yielding your heart, spirit and soul.

It's about being aligned with the will of God and picking up heaven's frequency.

> 'Routine puts you in a place where you worship from the outer court while relationship takes you beyond the veil.'

Routines make you worship the unknown, relationship opens your eyes to the realities of the God you know.

Ignorant worship informs you about a God, and the ignorant worshipper has no knowledge of who that God is.

Ignorant worship has all the attributes of worship but has no depth or substance as the worshipper and the worshipped do not come together. Therefore, no correlation exists.

Theory and practice do not come together, and as a result, the worshipper remains alienated to the worshipped.

Acts 17:23-31 we see the worshipper deep in worship to an unknown god:

> 'Now as I was going along and carefully looking at your objects of worship, I came to an altar with this inscription: 'TO AN UNKNOWN GOD.' Therefore what you already worship as unknown, this I proclaim to you.'

It is possible for this to happen Jesus told the woman at the well that Samaritans worshipped what they did not know.

'You [Samaritans] do not know what you worship; we [Jews] do know what we worship, for salvation is from the Jews.'

John 4:22

Strive to know the God you worship!

4. True Worship

This is a type of worship that is void of gimmicks, carnality, hypocrisy, entertainment, pride, vain glory, selfish agenda and self-gratification.

It is not focused on showmanship and the attainment of celebrity status, nor does it concern its self with outward appearances, politics in the worship team and manipulation strategies to ensure you are in the limelight and all those ungodly practices that go on within the worship circle.

These are practices that repel people from joining worship teams, attend churches or associate with 'Christians.' These practices are the order of the day in some churches, house fellowships, gatherings and even our hearts!

True worship occurs when there is a connection with God.

It comes from a place of revelation of who God is.

It transcends beyond the state of your voice or the availability or not of instruments.

It is not hindered by the lack of money or talent.

You do not need to have a crowd present, and it is not influenced by any human being's opinion.

You need to get to a place where you would not be sucked in by all those distractions that rob us from standing naked before our maker.

True worship occurs in a state where you are naked, and you are not ashamed!

This is the reason why God could go down and fellowship with Adam and Eve every day in the Garden of Eden. They enjoyed their worship time which resulted in attracting the presence of God, this continued until they got distracted and shifted the focus on themselves and what they can become; after this had happened all they could see was their nakedness and not God's glory!

As a result, they forgot God's ability to see them and see through them. They were so engrossed in 'self' that their focus moved from God to what they could achieve with all this new found power.

They focused on how they could rise up to unimaginable heights and what they could do with this new power rather than God's grace and favour. They even thought and felt the need to hide from God!

If your worship provokes the need to mask your identity and try to be someone else. If your worship incites the need to hide behind things that gratify your flesh. If your worship exposes your nakedness and you cannot stand bare before your maker due to the state of your heart then it is not true worship!

You should be able to stand naked before your maker without any masks in worship because all we need to make us whole is the power that is in the blood of Jesus. This is our one plea. It is the blood that sanctifies and redeems not your work of righteousness or your 'professionalism' or whatever criteria that we have been deceived to believe matter.

> 'But a time is coming and is already here when the true worshippers will worship the Father in spirit [from the heart, the inner self] and in truth; for the Father seeks such people to be His worshippers 24 God is spirit [the Source of life, yet invisible to mankind], and those who worship Him must worship in spirit and truth.'
>
> *John 4: 23-24*

'True worship is not man-centred!'

We are encouraged to come to Him in reverent praise and prayers not hide away from Him.

> 'O come, let us worship and bow down, Let us kneel before the LORD our Maker [in reverent praise and prayer].'
>
> *Psalm 95:6*

God is interested in us and the worship we bring in Hebrew 13:15. We learn that God wants us all to approach Him at all times through our saviour Jesus Christ.

> 'Through Him, therefore, let us at all times offer up to God a sacrifice of praise, which is the fruit of lips that thankfully acknowledge and confess and glorify His name.'

Your worship cannot be true if you are a fornicator or adulterer, a thief, a slanderer, a brawler, if you are full of anger and hatred, if you are proud and arrogant, full of selfish ambition, a hypocrite, a backbiter, full of impure thoughts, remember your nakedness will be highlighted before God (1Corinthins 6:9) God is not mocked.

You may be able to cover up and deceive those in your social circle and circle of influence but remember you are naked before God!

If you are naked and ashamed, then ask for help remember God is ready to cover you, God is not calling for perfect people and is aware that we are imperfect beings created in His image.

God is willing to work with you to make your relationship with Him valuable, acceptable and worthwhile.

There is an open invitation:

> 'Come now, and let us reason together,' Says the LORD. 'Though your sins are like scarlet, They shall be as white as snow; Though they are red like crimson, They shall be like wool.'
>
> *Isaiah 1:18*

True worship flows because it is led by the Holy Spirit. It's all about worshipping God in Spirit and in truth.

> 'Whenever the living beings moved, the wheels moved with them; and when the living beings rose from the earth, the wheels rose also. [20] Wherever the spirit went, the beings went in that direction. And the wheels rose along with them; for the spirit or life of the living beings was in the wheels.'
>
> *Ezekiel 1:19-20*

In true worship we drink from the river whose streams make glad the city of God (Psalm 46:4), true worship produces life, fruitfulness, healing, wherever the river goes.

> 'It will come about that every living creature which swarms in every place where the river goes, will live. And there will be a very great number of fish, because these waters go there so that the waters of the sea are healed and become fresh; so everything will live wherever the river goes.'
>
> *Ezekiel 47:9*

When we worship God is spirit and in truth, we produce results, our declarations are honoured, our prayers are answered just like Jesus did at the tomb of Lazarus. He worshipped, declared and was honoured.

True worship glorifies God!

May we focus on worship that glorifies God and God alone in Jesus name amen!

Chapter 5

Here I Am to Worship

*'But you have come to Mount Zion and to the city o the living
God, the heavenly Jerusalem, and to myriads of angels [in festive
gatherings] and to the general assembly of the firstborn who are
registered [as citizens] in heaven, and to God, who is Judge of
all, and to the spirits of the righteous (the redeemed in heaven)
who have been made perfect [bringing them to their final glory].
And to Jesus, the Mediator of a new covenant [uniting God and
man], and to the sprinkled blood, which speaks [of mercy], a
better and nobler and more gracious message than the blood of
Abel [which cried out for vengeance].'*

Hebrews 12:22-24

I am sure by now you have decided to make key adjustments and developments to your worship life.

This is a deep revelation that is helping me on a daily basis, and it would be an error not to share it with the world.

Naturally, the progressive step to take is to enquire when one can offer true worship to Elohim. The answer is at all-time hence the talk earlier of living a worship lifestyle.

However here are some prescribed ways for those who like to follow a pattern.

When You Are Happy

You need to remember to offer praises and thanksgiving to God when you are happy. The author of Psalm 95:2 shows us that we do not only need to have a one-sided relationship with God where all we do is take; he implores us saying

> *'Let us come before His presence with a song of thanksgiving; Let us shout joyfully to Him with songs.'*

In Psalm 103:1 we see David express his gratitude for God's mercies

> *'Bless and affectionately praise the LORD, O my soul, And all that is [deep] within me, bless His holy name.'*

Sometimes we just need to come and worship Him just because we can. We should get to a place in life where we can just offer grateful praise and:

> *'declare His glory among the nations, and His marvellous works and wonderful deeds among all the peoples'*
>
> *Psalm 96:3*

This definitely makes Satan the enemy to fear!

We must learn to praise God in advance because we understand that he is faithful to us and does not slumber nor sleep concerning us. We must always find a new song and offer to Him in worship. He is worthy!

> *'He put a new song in my mouth, a song of praise to our God; Many will see and fear [with great reverence] And will trust confidently in the LORD.'*
>
> *Psalm 40:3*

At All Times

Worshipping God at all times is a choice and could be sacrificial.

You do not need a specific reason or occasion to worship because God is constant. He is the only constant being. Habakkuk 3:17-18 teaches us to choose to lead a worship lifestyle irrespective of our internal and external influences or circumstances he states:

> *'Though the fig tree does not blossom And there is no fruit on the vines, Though the yield of the olive fails And the fields produce no food, Though the flock is cut off from the fold And there are no cattle in the stalls, 18 Yet I will [choose to] rejoice in the LORD; I will [choose to] shout in exultation in the [victorious] God of my salvation!*

David got this revelation at a very turbulent time in his life. The king was after his life, it was public knowledge that the king was unequivocally determined to assassinate David whatever the cost. He was on the hunt for David, and this caused David to live like a fugitive. David ran into the home of Abimelech, the priest and saw the hand of God in action.

David left the presence of the priest with food and the sword of Goliath.

David also wrote:

> *'I will bless the LORD at all times;*
> *His praise shall continually be in my mouth.'*
> *Psalm 34:1*

You are at liberty to worship all day and all night, every second of your life should be lived as a sacrifice of worship. The only restrictions are those placed by you. Psalm 113:3 tells us that God is enthroned and worthy of worship always.

> *'From the rising of the sun to its setting, The name of the LORD is to be praised [with awe-inspired reverence].'*

You can worship in your bed Psalm 149:5

> *'Let the godly ones exult in glory;*
> *Let them sing for joy on their beds.'*

103

Early in the Morning Time

It is a good habit to form. As a parent I teach my children to say something nice in the morning. They have to say a greeting and ask how the night went. This I find is a way of bonding and getting motivated for the day.

You might not have the best work colleagues or meet the greatest people when you leave the house, but if you started on a positive note, then you will have that spring in your step to help you make a great fresh start just as the psalmist advises us to awake and call forth our glory.

> *'Awake, my glory! Awake, harp and lyre! I will awaken the dawn.'*
>
> *Psalm 57:8*

Psalm 3:3 tells us that God is our glory and the lifter of our heads.

Sacrifice in the Midnight Hour

The midnight hour is the darkest hour of our lives, and at this hour it is very easy to lose focus, this is a good time to sow worship in faith. This is a good hour to hold on to God's word because joy is round the corner.

It is not a time to focus on the hour but to focus on the morning which is a second away. God promises us joy in the morning, so it is a time to worship in anticipation of the imminent joy!

Here is the secret of midnight worship; God does not despise sacrifices from a broken and a contrite heart therefore, you are guaranteed an answer!

So take advantage of His word and go ahead and offer a sacrifice of worship even in that midnight situation and remind God that He does not despise such sacrifices.

He is a faithful and just God who honours His word.

> *'For You do not delight in sacrifice, or else I would give it; You are not pleased with burnt offering. ¹⁷ My [only] sacrifice [acceptable] to God is a broken spirit; A broken and contrite heart [broken with sorrow for sin, thoroughly penitent], such, O God, You will not despise.'*
>
> *Psalm 51: 16-17*

The author of Psalm 119 tells us to rise up in the midnight hour, to rise above the issues of the midnight hour and give God who is our author and finisher; who has us engraved in the palms of his hands, who has good thoughts for us to bring us a hope, and a future, thanks instead of moaning.

In verse 62 of Psalm 119, the Psalmist informs us that:

> *'At midnight I will rise to give thanks to You Because of Your righteous ordinances.'*

You can go to him in worship when you need to battle, and he will train your hands to war and your fingers to battle and cause you to escape just like he did for David. (Battle examples have been given in the earlier chapters)

When You Feel Down

Some people live daily with mental health challenges and need specific and supervised help. This is a very serious illness and is no respecter of status. There has been an increased awareness of depression within the church, and the advice that comes from me is to seek medical help as soon as you think it is the case.

We need to be able to get to a point where we can differentiate between feeling down and needing help. We need to look out for each other. There have been suicides within the church due to missed opportunities to observe or question signs. Many Christians are still not being open about depression, stress related illnesses and mental health related illnesses. Too many people are still living with depression refusing to seek professional help and be open. Far too many people are still suffering in silence when it should not be!

There is no shame in seeking help if you or a loved one is suffering and it's about time that the stigma should be taken off from the pews to the back rows. Our approach will be different if the individual was diagnosed with cancer but this is worse as it is a 'hidden' illness which is known mostly to the sufferer.

On the other hand, if you do not have mental health challenges, need I say it is part of life to feel down because we are all creatures of emotion and our emotions fluctuate all the time.

As living beings, one of our characteristics is to respond to stimuli.

There is nothing bad in having emotions however we need to be in a position where we can manage our emotions. I would like to announce to you that emotions are very challenging to manage; however, we can choose to accommodate them, challenge them, use them, be used by them or simply put our lives in perspective against them.

The unnamed author of Psalm 42 and 43 goes through a process when faced with despair.

We see him plunge down into a dark emotional state and analyse the challenge he was facing at the time. He does not stop there but goes ahead to take stock of what has happened and look ahead to see if there is any light at the end of the tunnel.

Further, he also arms himself with the word, confronts the misery he is facing with the word, then seeks God's help in faith (believing he is able to come out) and finally, he worships God for the result he is hoping for!

As you can see, there are many steps taken by the troubled writer!

But the good news is we are more than conquerors and overcomers in Christ Jesus.

So whatever situation you find yourself in, ensure you seek help and believe God for victory.

> *'These things I [vividly] remember as I pour out my soul;*
> *How I used to go along before the great crowd of people and*
> *lead them in procession to the house of God*
> *[like a choirmaster before his singers,*
> *timing the steps to the music and the chant of the song],*
> *With the voice of joy and thanksgiving, a great crowd*
> *keeping a festival.*
> *Why are you in despair, O my soul? And why have you become*
> *restless and disturbed within me?*
> *Hope in God and wait expectantly for Him, for I shall again*
> *praise Him For the help of His presence.'*
>
> Psalm 42:4-5

When You Need to Meet with God

We serve an omnipresent God. However, we still need to seek His face. God is near, but we can choose to distant Him from us and put Him out in the garden while we carry on partying inside the house.

The great thing is that He has promised never to leave us nor forsake us.

He has promised to always cause His face to shine upon us so whenever you feel the need to meet with your father just go to Him in worship. He loves it and has promised to dwell in the words that you bring to Him in praise and adoration.

What is stopping you! Even the troubled Psalmist in Psalm 42:2 understood the importance of meeting God for a heart to heart.

> *'My soul (my life, my inner self) thirsts for God, for the living God.*
> *When will I come and see the face of God?'*

You can see the face of God whenever you decide to because He will not hide his face from us when we live according to his will. We only get separated from Him by sin. Sin causes a wedge to be drawn and brings separation.

Make the decision today to live right and have full access to Elohim at all times. Psalm 24:3-4 has the criteria for seeking His face

'Who may ascend onto the [a]mountain of the LORD?
And who may stand in His holy place?
4 He who has clean hands and a pure heart,
Who has not lifted up his soul to what is false,
Nor has sworn [oaths] deceitfully.'

When you need to see His face in the midst of pain or when you need to rejoice, we are instructed by James to pray and offer praises.

'Is anyone among you suffering? He must pray. Is anyone joyful?
He is to sing praises [to God].'
James 5:13

Even when God says no you must still worship because God is just. King David had done wrong before God, and the judgement had been issued. God was not pleased with David and David recognised and accepted God's judgement and still worshipped.

When you have done wrong, and the consequences catch up with you be humble enough to worship instead of holding a grudge against God for allowing the consequences catch up with you. This is what David did:

'Then David got up from the ground, washed, anointed himself
[with olive oil], changed his clothes, and went into the house of the
LORD and worshipped. Then he came [back] to his own house,
and when he asked, they set food before him and he ate.'
2Samuel 12:20

When in Trouble

This is what Jonah did in the belly of the fish, he knew he was in trouble and needed God. He ended his prayer in worship acknowledging that he can only get salvation from the Kind and Saviour of the universe.

'But [as for me], I will sacrifice to You
With the voice of thanksgiving;
I shall pay that which I have vowed.
Salvation is from the LORD!'

Chapter 6

How Can I Worship?

Worshipping God is beyond talent or being part of any band/ worship team as you can only worship with the help of the Holy Spirit. In 1Chronicles 29:14 we are made to understand that everything comes from God.

Jesus promised to not leave us without a guide or a comforter, it is possible to lead a worship lifestyle as long as you depend on the Holy Spirit to help you.

> 'For from Him [all things originate] and through Him [all things live and exist] and to Him are all things [directed]. To Him be glory and honour forever! Amen'
>
> *Romans 11:36*

He is indeed the source of even our worship. When John the Baptist was questioned about Jesus' anointing by some people who doubted the integrity of Jesus John replied

> 'A man can receive nothing [he can claim nothing at all] unless it has been granted to him from heaven [for there is no other source than the sovereign will of God.'
>
> *John 3:27*

Ask the Holy Spirit for help, and you will see how easy it is to touch God's heart in worship.

Without Condemnation or Guilt

Given we have an accuser (Satan is the accuser of the brethren), for your worship to be acceptable; it must come from a place void of condemnation or guilt. In criminal law, for you to win, the burden of proof must be beyond the reasonable doubt. If the jury thinks there is an iota of doubt, you cannot be exonerated, and the prosecution will do all they can to point out your guilt!

So it is with our prosecutor who is Satan, he will do all he can to demonstrate your guilt and your need for condemnation, however, there is hope because we understand that salvation bring us righteousness and we have been set free from bondage.

'There is now no condemnation [no guilty verdict, no punishment] for those who are in Christ Jesus [who believe in Him as personal Lord and Saviour]'

Romans 8:1

Your righteousness must come from God through faith in Jesus Christ to all who believe.

'Unlike the accuser, Jesus came to save and not to condemn so stop condemning yourself of past sins that have been deleted from God's database.'

'For God did not send the Son into the world to judge and condemn the world [that is, to initiate the final judgment of the world], but that the world might be saved through Him.'

John 3:17

'Jesus is the Lord our righteousness, true righteousness is not earned but received by faith so approach your maker and go beyond the veil in worship.'

Romans 3 21-22 clearly states:

'But now the righteousness of God has been clearly revealed [independently and completely] apart from the Law, though it is [actually] confirmed by the Law and the [words and writings of the] Prophets. 22 This righteousness of God comes through faith in Jesus Christ for all those [Jew or Gentile] who believe [and trust in Him and acknowledge Him as God's Son]. There is no distinction.'

However, this is not a licence to live in sin as God is not mocked, whatever you do every second of the day, make sure you do not nail Jesus back to the cross!

Shout and Clap

You can worship with a shout!

If you are not musically talented, do not let this hinder you as God is not interested in your key so just go ahead and make a joyful noise unto the Lord! Yes, you can worship with a shout! In Joshua 6, the children of God were specifically instructed by God to shout, not just to make a loud sound but to utter a battle cry out against the walls of Jericho.

When you shout out in worship, remember you are doing warfare against the walled town and high towers that have exalted themselves against the knowledge of God in your life.

When you have no words to say, and you are in the midst of the storms and against those walls cry out in worship! When you do not know the lyrics clap your hands and shout for joy, don't just stand there and look around participate when you are in a worship gathering.

'O clap your hands, all you people; Shout to God with the voice of triumph and songs of joy.'
Psalm 47:1

You can also make audible worship sounds by clapping your hands and using them as a musical instrument as instructed by the sons of Korah to the chief Musician when exalting God and acknowledging Him as the King of the earth.

Psalm 98 is a call to praise the Lord for His righteousness, the psalmist instructs the seas to thunder and roar, the rivers to clap their hands and the mountains to sing for joy and delight. Oh, what a picture!

In Isaiah 55:12, even the mountains and the hills are said to have the ability to break forth into shouts of joy and the trees exhibit the ability to clap their hands before those who are led by the Lord

Do what you can to give audible worship to the Lord remember He has the ability to raise stones to give Him praise if you refuse to worship.

Lift up Holy Hands

You can worship the King by demonstrating your servitude and submission. You can show Him you surrender and that you are laying down all you are and all you know and stand for by lifting up holy hands to Him and kneeling down before His Eminence.

In Nehemiah 8, there was a meeting scheduled for the reading of the book of the law and the stage was set for this purpose. The people sat there from morning till midday listening to the word and in verse 8 they responded to the word in worship. They responded to God with their worship by demonstrating they were under His rulership and awesome power. They abased themselves in worship. They were there to receive from the bread of life, but they also gave their lives in worship.

'Then Ezra blessed the LORD, the great God. And all the people answered, 'Amen, Amen!' while lifting up their hands; and they knelt down and worshipped the LORD with their faces toward the ground.'

Nehemiah 8:6

When Apostle Paul was instructing Timothy on worship, his first instruction was that prayers and thanksgiving should be made for those in positions of leadership and authority and he explained that God takes pleasure in this type of prayer. His second instruction was the lifting up of holy hands.

'Therefore I want the men in every place to pray, lifting up holy hands, without anger and disputing or quarrelling or doubt [in their mind].'

1 Timothy 2:8

David also worshipped with his hands lifted up.

'So will I bless You as long as I live;I will lift up my hands in Your name.'

Psalm 63:4

'Let my prayer be counted as incense before You; The lifting up of my hands as the evening offering. The Psalmist in Psalm 134:2 appeals to the congregation to Lift up your hands to the sanctuary And bless the LORD.'

Psalm 141:2

Express Love for God with all Your Heart, Soul, Mind and Strength

The greatest commandment as we are told by Jesus himself in Mark 12:30 is to love the Lord our God with all our hearts, souls, minds and strengths.

This is a subjective and individual criteria that can be achieved purely on such basis.

Meaning I (and nobody on earth) cannot and do not have the tools to measure the validity of your worship!

Because worship is offered solely to God and is accepted exclusively by God, God alone has the scale to measure if your worship is with all your heart, soul, mind and strength.

In Revelation chapter 4 we are introduced to the four living creatures who express their love for God day and night and never stop saying:

'Holy, holy, holy, is the Lord God Almighty who was and is and
is to come.'

We are drawn into the scene where we see the 24 elders fall down in
worship before Him who sits on the throne and worship Him who
lives forever and ever. We see them lay down their crowns before the
throne and tell Him:

*'Worthy are You, our Lord and God, to receive the glory and the
honour and the power; for You created all things, and because of
Your will they exist, and were created and brought into being.'*

Ask the Holy Spirit to help you with this, seek His approval only and
make sure you empty out yourself and not hold anything back.

Kneel down, Bow down, Prostrate

The Apostle John had the awesome and sole privilege while on the
island of Patmos to get an insight of what goes on in heaven. In the
book of Revelations 19:4, John sees the twenty-four elders and the four
living creatures fall down and worship God who sits on the throne,
saying,

'Amen. Hallelujah (praise the Lord)!'

There is a place for corporate kneeling down; in Psalm 95:6 the psalmist calls on the worshippers to all kneel and bow down before the King.

*'O come, let us worship and bow down,
Let us kneel before the LORD our Maker
[in reverent praise and prayer]'*

Psalm 2:11 also sends out the same message:

*'Worship the LORD and serve Him with reverence [with awe-in-
spired fear and submissive wonder]; Rejoice [yet do so] with
trembling.'*

Audibly — in Song, Music and Dance

There is a place for audible worship and inaudible worship. If you are able to speak you can use your voice, He gave you utterance for a reason David in Psalm 26:7 wrote thus:

'That I may proclaim with the voice of thanksgiving And declare all Your wonders.'

In Psalm 30, David wrote a Psalm for the dedication of the temple in this Psalm he used his voice and audibly cried, shouted, sang and even called upon his soul to sing out to God in worship.

In the book of Acts when the apostle Peter performed his first recorded miracle at the beautiful gate, the formerly lame man went into the temple leaping and audibly praising God.

There are also examples of people who praised with musical instruments and with a dance.

'Let them praise His name with dancing; Let them sing praises to Him with the tambourine and lyre.'
Psalm 149:3

You can also worship with audible sounds from a musical instrument such as the trumpet, harp, lyre, tambourine, stringed instruments, flute, cymbals, triangle, drums, accordion, xylophone, pipe, bells, and even glasses of water! (Psalm 150:3-5).

The sounds of instruments are prescribed and recognised by God when you do not use words to express your worship; the instrumental worship goes before God as warfare. In Numbers 10:9 the Lord gave an instruction regarding when the alarm from the 2 silver trumpets should be sounded. The Lord promised his people that the alarm sounded in time of war will cause the Lord to remember His people and save them from the hand of their enemy.

Instruments are very crucial in worship because their sound emits a battle cry before the Lord; their sound rises up in warfare against the enemy.

Inaudible Worship on Your Own

If, for whatever reason you are physically unable to worship audibly or create an audible sound, you can still worship Him inaudibly because it is with the mind that we serve the Lord. Or if you are in a place where you need to maintain silence, you can worship in your heart inaudibly.

You can always worship Him in your heart as an individual. You can let him know that you put your trust in Him and you love and adore Him.

He sees beyond outward appearances, beyond showmanship and any mask.

David in Psalm 27 declared his trust In the Lord in humble adoration and in verse 8 he responded to God with his heart

> 'my heart said to you, Your face, O Lord, I will seek (on the authority of Your word).'

Our thoughts are situated deep down in our hearts and minds, in places where only God can search out and reach, Psalm 150:6 commands everything that has breath and every breath of life to praise the Lord. When you are not able to praise him audibly, praise him in the depths of your heart and from the core of your being because He sees and hears those cries that flow from the fountains of our souls even when no one else is watching or is able to see.

Dance

You can also praise Him with a dance.

After the victorious exodus from Egypt, Miriam the prophetess and sister of Moses and Aaron lead the women in a worship dance procession Exodus 15:20-21.

Your dance could also execute judgement on those who mock you. In 2 Samuel 6, Michal made herself a mocker instead of joining in to offer a dance offering before the Lord. She is recorded to have remained barren till death. She did not share in the fruitfulness that was David's signature inheritance.

Don't spend your time looking around and judging people; instead join in and offer your own dance offering unto the Lord.

In the Midst of a Congregation

When in a congregation, you can worship corporately with the congregation at meetings, conferences and other gatherings of God's people. David declared:

'I will tell of your name to my country men, in the midst of the congregation I will praise you I will give you thanks in the great congregation I will praise you among a mighty people.'

Psalm 22:22

'It is your responsibility to declare God's glory everywhere you are; when on your own or when with people.'

Psalm 35:18

He is indeed worthy of praise!

A Sacrificial Act

You can also worship through an act of sacrifice.

Mary Magdalene fulfilled scripture unknowingly to her by her sacrificial act. In Matt 26.7 we see her worship the King by pouring the very expensive oil on Jesus' head at the table.

The story was elaborated in Luke 7:36. The writer described her act of worship and portrayed how she put her heart and soul into exalting the saviour with her wealth and dignity.

Job tore his clothes, shaved his hair, fell to the ground and worshipped God just in case his children had done wrong — Job 1:20.

You need to come to a place where you alone make a decision on the best way you can offer effective worship to Elohim.

Whatever you do ensure you are fulfilling your assignment, purpose and destiny which is worship.

God is still seeking those who worship Him in spirit and in truth; the question is will He find you?

Even the presence of angels, manifests fear in man.

The Bible is full of instances of angelic visitation which is always followed by the angels telling man to not be afraid!

This is because they reflect the glory that accompanies being in the presence of the Lord.

I leave you with this command:

'O worship the Lord in the beauty of holiness; tremble before and reverently fear Him, all the earth'

Psalm 96:9

End.

If you have been touched or affected by the words in this book and would like to be a disciple of the Lord Jesus Christ, all you need to do is ask Him to come into your life and take over.

After you have repented of your old ways, you need to find a bible believing church in your community and join so you can be baptised and supported in your journey.

You can also email me at j.d200@tiscali.co.uk with any questions and for coaching needs or find me on Facebook *delightsomeone ministries*

Remember God's grace is always sufficient!